LIFE,
the UNIVERSE,
GOD,
and all that
STUFF
(LUGS)

'an inside-out view'

by
JOHNNY R. O'NEILL

© 2018 *by* Johnny R. O'Neill

★★★

First digital edition August 2018
First print edition January 2019

Paperback ISBN: 978-0-578-42895-6

Over a lifetime, untold people have contributed to this project in ways little and ways big, and don't even know it. My thanks to all of them. Special thanks to my good friend Bob Waterman, my brother Kevin, and my daughter Kimie, for their thoughtful critiques, and cogent suggestions. And thanks, most especially, to my wife for her unwavering patience with a husband who has trouble concentrating on anything other than the project at hand, sometimes for, yeah, years on end.

Original cover art by Jeremy Page. Thank you Jeremy!

TABLE OF CONTENTS

TABLE OF CONTENTS *cont'd*

PREFACE

August 2018

'*The universe is the feeling of it.*'

Or, to put it more simply, 'the universe *is* feeling.'

It's tempting to use either phrase as an encapsulation of this book, but, what does it mean? Until we know what it means, and no matter how many times we repeat it, italicized or not, '*the universe is feeling,*' bolded or not, '**the universe is feeling,**' all caps or not, 'THE UNIVERSE IS FEELING!,' even with an exclamation point, until we know what it means…it doesn't mean a thing.

I'm not a philosopher. And I'm certainly not a physicist. I drive 'big rigs'; I've logged over a million miles in them. But, 'the road of life can get mighty rough, Son…,' that kind of 'sage wisdom'? That's not this book.

The first few chapters necessarily outline a little bit about me (I haven't always been a truck driver) as the book follows the chain of ideas that led me to make the leap, and it is a leap, to understanding that thoughts are feeling in the brain, smells are feeling in the nose, light is feeling in the eyes, and indeed, that 'eyes' are feeling, and 'brain' is feeling, and 'nose' is feeling, in short, that *life itself,* is feeling. Along the way, some of the mechanisms, some of our ideas of how our world 'works,' will be questioned, and some of the boundaries we use to define our world will get blurred.

As you read, do try not to get caught up in understanding every last assertion, argument, or line of

i

thought. It's like life, keep moving! Because (and again, like life) whatever it is that you're not getting, it's probably going to be covered again—and usually again and again—each time from a new perspective.

The ideas might seem (probably will seem) 'out there.' So, especially when first encountered, an initial 'suspension of disbelief'—like, when watching a sci-fi movie— might prove handy. My hope is that in the long run a kind of osmosis will take place. Ideas that will strike many of us as entirely outrageous, even absurd, when first we encounter them, will slowly start to seep in and begin to seem not so absurd, and maybe even perfectly reasonable. Not by repetition, but by explanation.

It happens.

To put it in the most simplistic of terms, I speculate (and again, *not* a physicist) that a class of subatomic particles called 'bosons,' the 'force carriers' of the subatomic world (photons, as an example, the 'particles' of light of our universe, they're bosons), act as little 'pinpoints' of feeling, and that by 'reading' the code of these pinpoints (coded by relative position, and held in place by the 'fermions' of the subatomic world), like reading the 'code' of these words, or like a computer 'reading' the ones and zeroes of computer code, that we experience, we live our world. Think of it like braille, for a universe. And more than that, much more than that, those bosons, they aren't separate from us, they *are* us.

Simple?

Maybe you think so. If you do, you'll be tempted to skip ahead (I'm guilty of doing that myself) to the crux of the matter. To save you some search time, it more or less begins in Chapter 8, with these words: *"There is nothing incorporeal, insubstantial, otherworldly, immaterial, in our kinetic whirl. If it exists, there is a reason for it to exist, as it exists, where it exists, in the condition in which it exists...."*

We're all valid; we all feel our way, making it up as we go along, but I think you'll miss something—you'll miss a lot—if you do skip ahead to that paragraph. It's a context thing, and *feeling* (and this won't be obvious), *feeling* is all about context, so, context is a big part of what this book is about.

Really, what this book is about, it's not encapsulated in the phrase, 'the universe is feeling,' because as we begin to understand that simple phrase, as the many implications of it begin to unfold...

It's not magic. It's not incorporeal, insubstantial, otherworldly, or immaterial. It's Life. *Everything* is Life. It's all around us. It *is* us.

U.S. Postal Service™
CERTIFIED MAIL® RECEIPT
Domestic Mail Only

For delivery information, visit our website at *www.usps.com®*.

PELHAM, NY 10803 OFFICIAL USE

Certified Mail Fee	$3.45		
$		$0.00	

0029
16

Extra Services & Fees *(check box, add fee as appropriate)*
- ☐ Return Receipt (hardcopy) $ $0.00
- ☐ Return Receipt (electronic) $ $0.00
- ☐ Certified Mail Restricted Delivery $ $0.00
- ☐ Adult Signature Required $ $0.00
- ☐ Adult Signature Restricted Delivery $

Postmark
Here

Postage
$2.47

$
Total Postage and Fees
$5.92

09/04/2018

ANCONIA STATION NEW YORK, NY
SEP - 4 2018

Sent To
Scharf Family
Street and Apt. No., or PO Box No.
266 Ancon Avenue
City, State, ZIP+4®
Pelham, NY 10803

PS Form 3800, April 2015 PSN 7530-02-000-9047   See Reverse for Instructions

Certified Mail service provides the following benefits:

- A receipt (this portion of the Certified Mail label).
- A unique identifier for your mailpiece.
- Electronic verification of delivery or attempted delivery.
- A record of delivery (including the recipient's signature) that is retained by the Postal Service™ for a specified period.

Important Reminders:

- You may purchase Certified Mail service with First-Class Mail®, First-Class Package Service®, or Priority Mail® service.
- Certified Mail service is *not* available for international mail.
- Insurance coverage is *not* available for purchase with Certified Mail service. However, the purchase of Certified Mail service does not change the insurance coverage automatically included with certain Priority Mail items.
- For an additional fee, and with a proper endorsement on the mailpiece, you may request the following services:
  - Return receipt service, which provides a record of delivery (including the recipient's signature). You can request a hardcopy return receipt or an electronic version. For a hardcopy return receipt, complete PS Form 3811, *Domestic Return Receipt*; attach PS Form 3811 to your mailpiece; for an electronic return receipt, see a retail associate for assistance. To receive a duplicate return receipt for no additional fee, present this USPS®-postmarked Certified Mail receipt to the retail associate.
  - Restricted delivery service, which provides delivery to the addressee specified by name, or to the addressee's authorized agent.
  - Adult signature service, which requires the signee to be at least 21 years of age (not available at retail).
  - Adult signature restricted delivery service, which requires the signee to be at least 21 years of age and provides delivery to the addressee specified by name, or to the addressee's authorized agent (not available at retail).
- To ensure that your Certified Mail receipt is accepted as legal proof of mailing, it should bear a USPS postmark. If you would like a postmark on this Certified Mail receipt, please present your Certified Mail item at a Post Office™ for postmarking. If you don't need a postmark on this Certified Mail receipt, detach the barcoded portion of this label, affix it to the mailpiece, apply appropriate postage, and deposit the mailpiece.

IMPORTANT: Save this receipt for your records.

PS Form **3800**, April 2015 *(Reverse)* PSN 7530-02-000-9047

1

BLURRING THE BOUNDARIES

September 2016

It was 1962, maybe '63, when I started this book.

I didn't know I'd started a book. I was six. We lived in New Jersey and my mom, a housewife, and my dad, then an upwardly mobile, young, executive at a high-profile company, had decided to join a church. Being my mom and dad, they chose the Unitarian Church.

What does it mean that we went to church for those three Sundays? What does it mean that I remember it? Not a vague memory either. Not one of those memories I have because there's a photo somewhere, so what I really remember is the photo, or because someone says, "Hey, remember that time…," but for me 'that time' is more haze than memory. No. The Unitarian Church, for me, is a crystal-clear moment in time…

We were walking, Mom and Dad to the left with my brother behind. That's how I remember it. And I wanted to go into the main hall, instead of to the Sunday school classroom, because I wanted to hear what the minister had to say, instead of learning how to write my name upside-down and backward in a mirror, which is what we actually did at that Sunday school. I remember that too.

I wanted to know about life, about the universe, about God, about everything! Standing there on that New Jersey sidewalk, on that Sunday morning, that's what I told my parents.

"Honey, it's not like that," said my mom, smiling down at me. "You'd be bored."

Kevin was a toddler, our youngest brother. "Kevin gets to go in!" I said. Silly argument, but at age six it was the only thing I could think to say. Maybe if I'd told them I was writing a book...

We only went to that Unitarian church for three Sundays, maybe two, before, I guess, my parents got bored. Three years later we moved to Illinois for two school years and three blissful summers. Then back to New Jersey for my seventh grade, then to Annapolis, Maryland for eighth, then to Florida where I started high school.

California is where I write this, where I now live, but when I get in a certain mood and think about the East Coast there's a deep, gut-level yearning I have for it, a feeling.

Probably just a childhood thing. But that's what this book is about, this book that I started on that New Jersey sidewalk, because, like most kids, I wanted to know about LUGS: life, the universe, God, and all that stuff! And my parents wouldn't let me in the main hall so I could hear about it first hand, from a minister.

Which of course is silly, but somehow I vividly remember that moment. And maybe that is what has prompted me, all my life since then, to keep my eyes open, my ears open, and learn all I could about LUGS, from *outside* the main hall.

And it's silly as well, or so it might seem, the conclusion I've come to after all these years. For what is life? To me?

A feeling.

Here's a feeling: Walking home from second grade, alone, and seeing the crossing guard in the middle of the

2

road in her yellow belt and hat, holding a transistor radio in one hand, waving you across with the other, tears running down her cheeks. Weird huh? And then five minutes later, coming home and seeing your mom, standing in the middle of the living room, watching the television, hand over her mouth, tears running down her own cheeks.

John F. Kennedy was dead, and 'assassinate' is not a nice word to learn at seven.

In so many ways I had a wonderful childhood. We lived in beautiful houses, in great neighborhoods. I had *my own sailboat* at age nine. It was only ten-feet long, but it was mine, and we lived on a lake. Wonder Lake! (Really, that was the name.) I sailed it every chance I got. More than once I had good Samaritan power-boaters insist on towing me home because they thought I was out in too big a breeze for my little boat. I knew I could get home, but they didn't. It was just that in the gusts, the boat would tip over, dunking me and my oversized life-jacket in the drink. Fun days!

Life is a metaphor of itself. In some way or another life reflects itself, everywhere. Wherever we look and whatever we feel, that something is reflected in some other place, in some other way, in some other manner, somewhere or other, elsewhere.

Language itself speaks of this. A house is often a sanctuary. So is a monastery. But a monastery isn't often a house. Life reflects things back and forth. We can't eat with a fork in the road, unless we stop and pick it up. Any given word in the dictionary is defined in terms of other words, which themselves are defined in terms of other words, which themselves... A rose by any other name would smell as sweet, but if it smells of oil, and is painted, is it a rose, or paint? If it is mere paint, is the ceiling of the Sistine Chapel mere plaster?

Life is a metaphor of itself. (It's the ultimate metaphor, really, because life *is* everything—that part is coming up).

The metaphor of my life, one of them, is the blurring of boundaries.

Four and a half years after learning that word, 'assassinate,' and collectively the nation got to learn it again. Twice. First for Martin Luther King, then for Robert F. Kennedy.

Later that same year I overheard a family friend, Pauly, nearly choking up with emotion describing to my dad a scene at the 1968 Democratic National Convention in Chicago, Illinois. "Jack, they were throwing baseballs, at *us* Jack, and they had nails, big nails, driven all the way through." Pauly was a Chicago *firefighter*.

I had seen the rioting on the television, and not just at that convention. We watched the news every night. Walter Cronkite on CBS, five nights a week intoning the number of dead and wounded, on both sides, in Vietnam. 'Huntley and Brinkley' on NBC, chronicling protests around the country. Anti-war protests. Civil rights marches.

Anyone who remembers the 1960s as the decade of peace and love, wasn't paying attention.

The country, *the world*, seemed to be coming apart. Riots in Watts. Rampant racism. The Ku Klux Klan. Segregated schools. Segregated housing. Gang warfare in the inner cities. Urban blight. Urban flight. Organized crime. Labor union corruption. Political corruption. The My Lia massacre: American soldiers murdering civilians, including children. The Cold War: ducking under desks for nuclear war drills. The world split, communism/capitalism. Airliners—dozens of airliners—hijacked to Cuba. Near monthly (no kidding) political/military coups in South America, Central America, Africa, Asia. Mass starvation in Africa. Serious discussion on the television about the limits of democracy; it seemed to only work in select Western nations, and maybe India (but they hadn't had it for long, so who knew). Pollution: Los Angeles was choking in smog; highways were awash in litter (seriously, litter, read 'garbage,' was everywhere on roadsides—my family's first TV set, no kidding, was a side-of-the-road rescue by my dad, who took it home and fixed it); a glance down the Delaware River from the Walt Whitman Bridge would show a string of tall smokestacks spewing black smoke; don't swim in Lake Erie; don't *touch* the water in the Delaware River. And as usual, the same old standbys: schools weren't doing their job; teachers and parents were coddling the kids; TV was ruining the kids; the country was morally corrupt; the national debt was out of control; politicians were ruining the country; bureaucracy was stagnating the country; small farms were being forced out of business; big business was taking over the world; the human race was being turned into office or factory automatons; other nations were taking advantage of us, especially France, which had lost all respect for us; Japan was stealing our technology; the Soviet Union was catching up to us; our military was losing its edge; the world was running out of oil, and food; China was a rogue nation that was going to start a nuclear war; communism was taking over the world!

But it was that scene with Pauly, my dad intently listening, momentarily ignoring the burgers sizzling on the grill on the patio, that brought it home to me in a very real way.

The world was not so big that even a lowly almost 12-year-old could hide from it.

Sometimes I feel like I've gone on a long journey, leaving by my front door, and after years of travel, on the road of my thoughts, I find that I've circled all the way 'round the long way, and now gaze at my own *back* door. All these years later I look across an open space, with nothing between me and my own back door but what amounts to a line in the sand.

That line in the sand might be called, 'consciousness: the feeling,' the *feeling* of what it is to be oneself, of what Life is, as yourself. It's the line that separates 'me' from 'not me.' I can't step across that divide and still be me.

So how, you might ask, having left by my front door, and traveled the world of my thoughts for so many years, can I now be looking at my back door, from the *other* side of that line in the sand that separates 'me' from 'not me'? How is that possible?

Because I never left out of the front door. It's the front door that is the weird one.

It's open. We can go out the front door of Life any time and explore all those wild and sundry and various things of our world. And no matter how far we go, no matter what the experience we've had, we've never left the house of our Life. We haven't even stepped beyond the threshold of our own front door, because wherever we may go, we take the house of Life with us.

'Life,' you may note, is now capitalized. I differentiate 'Life,' the thing that is, from 'life,' the thing we lead, because like the 'United States of America,' 'Life,' to me, is a thing—the only thing, as it turns out. If it exists in our world it is part of our house of Life, part of us, part of our *feeling* that is each of us, and that feeling that is each of us, is Life.

When we go out our front door of Life, every morning when we wake up we do it, and experience Life, all that we experience is now our house of Life. Our individual experience of Life. Not the thing 'itself.' The *experience* of the thing.

That's the mistake we make, continually, thinking in terms of 'things.' We are each an experience of being a thing, but outside of an experience of a 'thing,' there is no 'thing.' There is the experience; the feeling of being. We are the feeling of being a thing.

So, go out your front door of Life, or the back—it doesn't matter because the back then simply becomes the front (I used to live in a house where the back door was

the front door; I really did, in that house on the lake).
Go out, spend your day, and when you return (having,
of course, not really left), review the day and of the
many experiences you had that day pinpoint which, if
any, were not *your* experiences.

Any of them? Of course not.

If you experience your feet, you can feel them, that is
your experience, that is *you*.

If you experience your child, you can feel her/him
giving you a hug, or your puppy, or your coffee cup (I
do hug my coffee cups; I harbor deep feelings for them),
that is your experience; that is you. That coffee cup, the
experience of it, not the thing but the experience of the
thing, that is you.

When you gaze at the stars, oh-so-far away, how
could they be you? It's not 'them'; it's the experience of
them that is you. Your experience. The house of your
Life never leaves you. It is always there, always encompassing.

It is what you are. All of Life. Your Life.

I'm a young and brash sixty years old as I write this,
just turned, and it was a long journey, all the way 'round
to the back door of my house of Life. Any journey
worth the effort of it, like my own, they often don't
make sense, not at the time, they don't. But, that's Life,
and we soldier on anyway. And when we have a chance,
we look back at our world and try to make sense of it,
and try to make sense of our lives, and see if it makes
sense, for us, to be wherever we find ourselves.

I hope that's the way you 'live' this book, that at any
given point, whether it makes sense or not, soldier on!
Then later, if you need to, look back and make sense of
it, and see if, for you, it makes sense to be where the
ideas of this book do lead you.

Moving every year or two is tough on friendships.
More than that it's tough on a sense of 'place.'

There is no place I call 'home,' now. I live where I live, sure, but I don't think of myself as a Californian. I'm not a Floridian either, or a New Yorker (even if I was born there). I've lived in the East, the West, the South, the North, the Midwest. I've been a resident of nine different states. I'm a Yankee who is comfortable saying, 'Hey y'all!'

Yes, I'm middle-class, but that's a big place, and I've pretty much run the gamut of it. Grew up upper middle, or as close as could be. Then my dad started his own company and we became blue collar guys. I dug ditches in dirt, with shovels, side by side with my dad (for the first year anyway, before he could afford to hire a crew—when I dug with them) during the summer, and on many a weekend during the school year. Working outside in stultifying Florida heat we laid cable in trenches, on poles, on the side of buildings, in stifling hot attics and along wasp-infested eaves, in condos, schools, trailer parks, apartment buildings, even marinas under the docks. We even wired up Homestead Air Force Base (before Hurricane Andrew). Cable TV was the new thing.

We moved from our Solar Drive (since renamed Solar *Isle* Drive—it actually is an island) home in Fort Lauderdale, a 20-minute ocean breeze stroll from the beach, to a duplex in Coral Springs, a couple humid miles from the Everglades, to a trailer park in Margate, near the road noise of State Road 7. Along the way we gave up a beautiful house we had purchased in Homestead, Florida, my mom's dream home, in which she had wanted to live out the rest of her life, but instead only managed a year or two, to the bank. We did that because as a family, and as a nation, we learned a new acronym: OPEC, Organization of Petroleum Exporting Countries.

It was the oil crisis of 1973, and it hit South Florida, a region heavily dependent on tourism and construction (my dad's company), like (as my dad would say) a ton of bricks. Along with the rest of the country we learned how to wait in line for gas, and pay lots of money for it. For a brief period, before it became the new normal, life seemed to revolve around the state of our gas tanks. Three-quarter full, still breathing, but looking for a station with gas and no line. Half a tank start worrying. Quarter tank and you're losing sleep. Eighth of a tank and the good life is all but flashing before your eyes. Less than that and you're looking at sleeping in line at the gas station. In your car.

Everyone had gas cans in their trunk. Teenage kids, high-heel divas, fat old guys in leisure suits with white belts and matching shoes (this was Florida), they were all pulling out gas cans to fill them up.

Lucky me, I missed most of the financial turmoil my family went through. I joined the navy.

There is no 'class' in the military, except for officer and enlisted. I was enlisted. A squid. Also a bubblehead.

So, no economic class, except I was never so poor I went hungry. No social class, except I was never so rich I belonged to a country club. No academic class or credential either, except for a genuinely excellent high school experience my final two years.

No geographical sense of place.

I am a baby boomer. Wherever a baby boomer goes, she/he is never there alone, and is usually scrambling to get the last seat, if any are left at all.

My parents were so disgusted with the state of the overcrowded public schools in growing-like-a-weed South Florida that they dug deep into their slowly emptying pocketbooks to send their eldest to a brand new, private high school (now closed) in the (then) small city of Coral Springs.

I am male. I am white. Not something I can ignore. I try not to let it define me.

I never was part of a religion. Other than that brief experiment with the Unitarian Church we never went to church. My wife and I have continued that tradition with our own family.

The whole world was once part of a tribe. Much of it still is. Not me. My name is O'Neill, third generation on my dad's side (third generation Swedish on my mom's), but I don't even think of myself as Irish, let alone Celt (or Viking!).

More than that, by descent I am European, not American. As a white man, I don't even belong here. Although I certainly don't belong in Europe either.

I don't belong, don't want to belong, to anywhere, to anything, except to my family as a father, husband, and brother, to my friends as a friend, to humanity as a human, to Earth as a mammal, and to the United States of America, as a citizen.

Others will define me, for themselves, in terms of boundaries that they themselves have defined and that exist for them around me. But, to me? I've erased most of the boundaries, or had them erased for me.

Hallelujah. I'm free!

2

PARTICLE/WAVE

October 2016

Getting a high school diploma is like getting a PhD in 'kid.' You're now a bona fide expert in being a kid, but instantly aren't one anymore. Might seem mean, but finishing something isn't about being 'done'; it means take a deep breath, let it out, and on to the next thing.

College, then, after getting that 'PhD,' is like preschool for adults. And I tried one, a great school, East Coast, brick and ivy, if not Ivy League. They taught me logic, the unadulterated variety. Symbols and rules. It was my first, my introductory, philosophy class, and I knew I'd be great at philosophy. For that first class, Logic, I had an excellent instructor. Understood his subject. Took the time to teach it. And I'm pretty sure it was a gift, when he gave me that 'C.'

It's not that I couldn't understand it; it's that I didn't want to understand it, not in all its exquisite complexity. I didn't see the point, and I was, frankly, appalled that Western philosophy placed so, so much importance on it. Because in my deep fount of 18-year-old wisdom (that's sarcasm, by the way), I knew that logic was not a key to Life. It didn't pave a path, or set a foundation. It didn't even point the way.

To me (although at the time I didn't look at it in these terms), the raw material of which we build the house that is our Life is not logic. Logic can be used to help square-up the framing, for example, that we use to hold up the roof. But the framing itself isn't made from logic, nor is it necessarily even square, or 'logical'—which doesn't mean it can't keep us dry.

Put another way, we don't build a house from our tools, we build it with our tools, but Western philosophy seemed, to me, built of nothing if not logic, of definitions and rules, and a lot of semantics.

Logic depends, utterly depends, on strict definitions, 'this is a footer,' 'this is a joist': that type of construction. In other words, it can only be utilized—the construction itself can only be deemed 'logical'—if it takes the form of a 'whole' composed of connected pieces, each connected piece of which is its own logically whole thing, a 'foot bone connected to a leg bone' kind of thing. But logic doesn't play well with constructions that aren't 'constructed,' constructions, in other words, that don't have 'boundaries,' that don't have pieces.

Weird kind of construction, maybe, a construction of no pieces, but, are you, am I, are we, no more than a series of pieces? Put together?

If I scrape the shingles off the roof of my house, the old, curling vinyl floor in the bathroom remains unchanged, as does virtually every other part of the house (please don't rain!). But, if I pull out Hildi from my house of Life, our family dog, a dachshund, all the three litters she had, watching them be born, sightless, helpless, watching my mom trying to save the runt, watching little Hildi laying on her side for hours on end nursing, nursing, watching the pups take over the house as they grew, watching people come over to pick out which ones they wanted when they were old enough, crying when they took away my favorites, all those times when short little Hildi would jump up on my bed in the middle of the night (when she was spry enough to do that!), laying right up against little Johnny and over the course of the night, night after night, pushing me all but off the bed...

Doesn't it seem likely that if Hildi could be magically taken away from me, it would change 'parts' of me *throughout* me? Parts that make me, me? Over the years I've changed in ways I never would have changed, if not for that 'Hildi part,' so, the way I look at it, the 'Hildi part' of me isn't complete unto itself. Tendrils of influence from that 'Hildi part' have seeped into nearly every aspect of my being in ways that could never be isolated and removed. Which says to me that 'Hildi' is a 'part' that *can't* be removed. Not if I'm to be me. Which makes Hildi not really a 'part,' but inherent to the whole.

My house lacking shingles is still my house, just lacking shingles. But me lacking little Hildi? There is no 'me' lacking Hildi. The 'me' that might remain is not me. Not at all.

So, when I squeezed out that 'C', in logic, and all my other classes were boring (except Russian, I liked that class, I was just no good at it, so another 'C')—especially next to the wonderful high school experience I'd had— when we had a fire in our rented house (now in Titusville, Florida), burning up nearly all the family pictures (and all the many 8mm home movies my dad had shot), it was time to call a permanent break from school and blame it, to all who might ask, on a fire. Handy!

One evening, I was maybe ten (I can get a fairly accurate read on my age at any point in memory based on which house we were living in), Dad and I were sitting on the porch and he asked me out of the blue, "Hey, Johnny, what time do you think it is, up there, on the moon?"

Dad was a tech guy, a self-taught electronics engineer—very little college (he attended Penn State, briefly). If someone introduced themselves to him as a PhD, and many did over the years, because he worked for a number of tech companies (most notably RCA, and briefly for Eckert-Mauchly) Dad was instantly on his guard. He had enormous respect for some PhDs, but found most worse than useless.

Just an old-fashioned, show-me-don't-tell-me, hands-on guy, right? Maybe. But he also studied physics. Einstein was his hero. He had an understanding of general relativity, had worked through much of the math for himself, so when he pointed out to his ten-year-old son that it's not the same time on the moon as it is on Earth, the explanation of how this could be was maybe a little advanced for the boy. Time dilation, speed of light, equivalence principle, Michelson-Morley experiment...and we're only getting started. Head explode kind of stuff. But yeah, ten years old, learning that it's not the same time on the moon as it is on Earth...

With the LUGS quest now on a back burner, working a cable job (not for Dad, who had no work), living with a roommate in Fort Lauderdale, in a haze of hormones, heat, alcohol (legal age in Florida was 18 at the time—not that it mattered, no one 'carded' anyway)—pulled by South Florida night-life and the ever-present, always calling but too rarely enjoyed, *heady* wine of young Florida women, it all conspired to leave me, young, active and vibrant, feeling that moment, *yay!*, but that moment?

It's a funny thing, but that kind of 'in the moment' existence where all things gel, where Life sizzles and the senses sing, *that* moment? It's great. It works. It's like the feeling of youth, right? Florida is good for that. Neon, heat, and sweat. But that's not the feeling you get trying to cross that line in the sand of your own backyard.

To feel *Life*, is to feel the totality, not only the sensual, not only the visual, but the place of it, the idea of it, the memory of it, the past future and present all at once of it, ensconced in it, inseparable from it, out of control buried in it, perfectly in control being it, being in the house of your Life. It's to feel you, and all your world, all at once, which 'you' can't do, because you can't consciously encompass all of you, the totality of you, and still be you, the 'you' you know.

It seems like it, but 'skin' isn't a boundary, not a boundary of 'me.' If it is a boundary, then why does it hurt when our doggy dies? The doggy is outside us, outside the skin we each call our own. How can it hurt inside our skin, for something that happens outside our skin?

We *have* to draw a line, somewhere, and be 'me' on one side, and 'not me' on the other, and we have to do that in order to exist at all, as anything. But the weird thing is that without the 'not me' part, the 'me' part doesn't exist, because that line in the sand of Life between 'me' and 'not me' only exists *because there is a place to draw it*. Which makes 'me' and 'not me' all the same thing.

Kind of like the 'wave-particle duality' that physicists have been grappling with for over a century now. There's the wave, like a light wave, exhibiting all the qualities of a wave, spreading out from a point, generating interference patterns upon encountering other waves. But then there is the particle, like a photon, a 'particle' of light with qualities that utterly distinguish it from a 'wave,' not 'propagating' but speeding straight ahead, and yet, light is both, 'particle' and 'wave.' A wave existing in all the places it could exist, a particle existing at the 'moment in time' that it is detected, a singularity that in one sense encompasses, and is itself encompassed by, the wave that it also exists as.

"Heavy man." That's what the guys in my dad's crew might have said, back in the '70s, hearing such an explanation. "It's like you're two things at once, man. Far out."

It's not heavy, man. It's not far out. It's one thing, each of us individually, being all that we are, all at once, existing inside a circle drawn in the sand of Life, which can't exist if there isn't all that sand in which to draw a line. All of which is what we are, all the time, anyway.

Abstractions, abstract ideas, to read them in a book, it's like reading sheet music. If we know the notes, if we can decipher the written code and hold it all in our head, we can hear it, but we'll only hear it in our head. Our head, alone.

To make music, real music, we have to *play* it. We have to sing it. The song being sung is like a wave. The notes being played are like particles. Particle/wave.

At the opera, we can detect the diva hitting all her notes, like her high C. But she's not 'singing' a high C. She's singing a *song*. An aria. The song is like a 'wave,' detected one 'particle,' one note, at a time. Particle/wave.

We can go to the Rocky Mountains, and hike to the top of a peak, and be there, at the Rocky Mountains, at one part of the Rocky Mountains. But not at all of it. The wave of a mountain range, detected on a particular peak. Particle/wave.

We can tell a story to our kid about our own childhood, and to that kid, hanging on our every word, experiencing us telling that story, the wave of our Life is being experienced by that kid via that story; but to us, that story is but one part of us, even a distant part, a particle. Our childhood encapsulated as a single story, a particle, experienced as a wave. Particle/wave.

It's not a mystery. It's not 'far out.' It is around us all the time. It's Life.

Dad could be infuriating. "Don't *try* to do it; *do* it." He said that a lot. And not in a friendly, understanding way.

So, that's what this book is. That's what I'm doing, not trying, *doing*, Dad I'm *doing* it, singing a song of my ideas, making a book about making a book about telling the tale of ideas and from whence they came, making a particle out of the wave of ideas, drawing a line in the sand of them and making the wave real.

Can you hear it?

The military is…wow. Kind of unexplainable.

I made two vows, the day I joined the navy. One was made with my right hand raised, standing before the flag, when aloud I swore allegiance to the United States of America and gave up my constitutional rights as a citizen of the U.S.A., to become subject instead to the UCMJ, the Uniform Code of Military Justice. The other vow I made moments earlier, silently, but that for me was just as solemn, just as real. I would do the six years of service that I'd signed up for; I wouldn't look back; I would give it the best I had, but after those six years I would get out, and again, I wouldn't look back.

That's what I did, and I haven't looked back. But, six years? At the time? It seemed like *forever.*

I hardly recognize myself in the few post boot camp photos I have. Buzz cut hair. The first day at boot camp, indeed the first hours, right after we got our hair cut, and then our uniforms, we packed the remnants of civilian life in a box, shoes, clothes, everything, sealed it, addressed it to home, and mailed it.

Then, some three days after she'd sent her son off to the navy, my mom received that box, no return address on it, opened it, and told me later that it hit her hard, that it was like she'd lost her eldest son.

She kind of did.

I was three. Maybe four. I was in the hallway of our Ashland house, at the corner of the back way leading to the kitchen; I can place it *exactly.* The house was bright with sunlight. Suddenly, there was Mom, or her legs anyway, and I looked up and she was smiling down at me and everything was perfect: "Mommy, you're the best mommy I ever had!"

I meant every word.

"But Honey," she said, smiling, "I'm the only mommy you've ever had."

"Oh."

That made *no* sense to me. And I can still feel how I felt, a sharp kind of, 'that's not right,' incredulity. But on the other hand, and suddenly, what she said made perfect sense to me, and I was wondering how I could have felt the other way, that she *wasn't* my only mommy?

Particle/wave.

Before we moved to Illinois, leaving the East Coast behind—forever, as far as anyone knew—Mom took us on a series of history tours. Over the few months before we moved we did the Liberty Bell, Valley Forge, Admiral Dewey's flagship, and more. The neighbor kids would come too, and their moms. We'd all pile in the family station wagon, a '58 Chevy, moms in the front seat, kids everywhere else, climbing over each other. No seat belts in those days. No car seats.

We waited in a long line and got a tour of the White House, and saw Lincoln's bedroom. We did the Smithsonian, and the Washington, Lincoln, and Jefferson Memorials/Monuments. We did Mount Vernon, and Monticello. We did Fort McHenry, of *The Star-Spangled Banner*, fame, and toured Brandywine Creek battleground, not far from where Mom grew up in Media, Pennsylvania. I still remember looking out over a field and imagining soldiers, dying there. And I still tear up, embarrassingly often, when I hear that refrain, '*and the flag was still there.*'

You learn stuff about the world. Like that Washington lost battles, a lot of them. That's news to a nine-year-old. At nine, heroes are supposed to win, not lose.

Dads are like particles. When they are there, they are *there*. Unmistakable. They take up space. They have momentum. We can see them and measure them, quantify them, remember them. My dad, anyway.

But moms? Moms are like waves. They inhabit our life in every way, without us even knowing it. They are everywhere at once, and nowhere in particular. They *never* go away. My mom, anyway.

3

Absolute Responsibility

October 2016

The navy settled me down. It was busy. Filled with stuff. Schools. Regulations. Personnel inspections (shoes shined, no hair touching ears). New people. New places.

It took some time to get my bearings and settle in, but the 'quest' was on.

I discovered 'Eastern' philosophy. Buddhism. Hinduism. Zen. Tao. I bought a copy of the New English Bible (I still have it) and read it, every word (except for the 'begats,' and, yeah, *Revelations*, I skimmed a lot of that).

I kept trying to find my way into Western philosophy, but reading Western philosophy is like opening a door to a vast castle of rooms and doors and twists and turns, and very few windows. Even if you do develop in your head a feeling for it, for knowing your way around, you're still stuck with a cold and unfurnished castle that was built as much or more as a defensive position against those who would assail it from the outside with their own logic, as it is a house in which you can reside safely within the walls of the builder's ideas.

But neither could I find my way into Eastern philosophy. Indeed, you don't so much find your way in, as find yourself unleashed from any sense of the familiar. Where the West is concerned with definitions, the East is often more concerned with erasing all definition. Yin and Yang. Koans. Which of course is a gross oversimplification, on both accounts.

The trouble was not with the books, or their authors. The trouble was with me.

You could say I was collecting ideas. But I think it's more accurate to say that I was rejecting ideas. That was the problem. I wasn't finding anything that made sense.

Ideas are like bells. They should ring true. I would read these ideas, and strike the bell of them in my head, to hear them fall flat or dead, tinny or weak. All of them! Until one day, in the most unlikely of books...

I was a navy 'nuke.' And it was two years of school the navy sent me to, including nuclear power school in Orlando, Florida, and prototype qualifications in Windsor Locks, Connecticut, before I reported to the fleet, to a Thresher-class fast-attack submarine based at the Point Loma submarine base in San Diego, my first and only boat.

I mention this because, being a nuke, and a submariner, you develop an appreciation that when it comes to the nuts and bolts of Life, all the good intentions and good ideas in the world won't amount to a hill of beans if you don't have all the pieces in place, fueled up, oiled up, aired up, ready to go.

It's a kind of systems engineering approach to thinking. The navy taught us math, including basic calculus. We learned chemistry. We learned heat transfer and fluid flow. We learned standard Newtonian physics, and nuclear physics as it applied to fission reactors.

But we also learned systems. We learned about steam engines. And things like condensers, and pressurizers, and types of pumps and motors and motor controllers and valves and piping systems, the list goes on and on.

Things work together. Systems work together. Systems are interlinked with each other. The weakest part determines the strength of the whole.

More than that, nothing exists in a vacuum. Put another way, everything exists in context. Put still another way, if a thing exists, there is a reason for it to exist, as it is, where it is, in the condition in which it is.

There is a reason. A contextual reason.

A character called Don Juan, in a book by a rather controversial author named Carlos Castaneda, spoke of responsibility for oneself—*absolute* responsibility. Unswerving, unmitigated responsibility for everything about oneself, *every* detail, *every* event.

Like I said, ideas are like bells. They should ring true. And the bell of that idea, the idea of absolute responsibility for oneself, from an author controversial or not, from a character perhaps fictional, perhaps not, rang true for me like no other idea I had ever heard before. (And indeed, for me that bell hasn't stopped ringing, and over the years has become nothing if not more and more melodious.)

It was also, at the time, a complete surprise. 'I am responsible for my life'? What does that mean!

I didn't trust it, at first. I didn't believe it at first. It didn't seem to fit my systems mode of thought, and yet here it was, ringing true. I kept wondering how it could make any sense, at all, that anyone was responsible—to take even the most basic of examples—for the circumstance of, say, their birth. *It made no sense.* And yet, somehow the idea rang true.

What kind of a 'truth' is it that makes no sense? I didn't know what to think about it. I was still in my early 20s, a very young man. I read a bunch more about this guy Don Juan but eventually gave up and put those books aside. For me there was just that one, shining idea, a beacon of an idea, but one I didn't know what to make of.

'Responsibility' is a causational word, a word that relies on 'things,' connections, hierarchies, abilities, and so on. It's a word with specific meanings and real implications. It's also a word I've been thinking about for 35 years, and about which I've come to some conclusions: For the time being, let's remove it from the phrase, 'I am responsible for my Life.' If we remove it, the phrase becomes simply, 'I am my Life.'

To 'be' your Life (as in, 'I am my Life'), is to be your Life in total. It's to not give your Life away, not any part of it. But what does it mean to not give your Life away?

It means to not give away, as an example, Hildi.

Hildi wasn't my dog. I didn't pick her out. I didn't ask for her. She was my mom's dog. So, not my 'fault.' Hildi's pups: not my 'fault.' Pushing me off the bed every night: not my fault, not my responsibility. *Separate.*

If that's the way I were to think about little Hildi, that she was separate, not part of me, not my 'fault,' then I would be giving part of me away. The pups, playing with them, watching them grow, watching little Hildi being a mom, like my mom, learning to understand things like being a mom but from another perspective, learning the value of Life, the joy of Life, those little things...

And it's so easy to think, of course Hildi is part of my Life. Why would I give Hildi away? Why would I call her 'not me'?

Why call the circumstances of birth or childhood, 'not me'?

Why call a disease, or disability, 'not me'?

Why call a body shape, 'not me'?

Why call a tragic error, 'not me'?

To repudiate the circumstance into which we are born, or 'who' we were born 'as,' or the circumstance in which we may find ourselves at any instance, is to repudiate a part of our Life. It is to take the experience that is 'me,' and call it 'not me,' fooling ourselves into thinking we're something we are not.

If, in accepting the experiences of our life as who we are, we refuse to let those experiences define us, or not, inform us, or not, limit us, or not—well, that too, is who we are, our individual experience.

There is more, much more, to the idea of 'absolute responsibility.' When you delve into it, it becomes obvious to the open eye what that notion is built upon. It's very simple, really. And it is that basis that is the reason why the idea of 'absolute responsibility' rang so very, very true for me for so long, and still does.

But, truly, I am a very slow thinker. I hate shortcuts of thought. I always want to go back and start over. Anytime new information, new ideas present themselves, I want to go back and re-think, re-purpose the whole thing, to see where that new idea fits and to see if there are any old ideas or old assumptions that maybe that new idea short circuits, but if we don't need that old idea, why did we have it in the first place? What was it there for? So, I'm going back further, and re-thinking the old idea.

It tends not to end. Which is why sane people invent shortcuts, jumping from idea to idea without going through all the interim steps.

So, as a simplistic example, you walk in the house on a Friday and the TV in the living room is on, and based on that single observation, you know you won't be going out tonight. Two ideas that, in your head, are directly linked to each other: 'TV on,' and 'no date.'

It's a no-brainer, for you, but only because you've short-circuited all the interim steps. You don't have to think about them. Dad's car, but not Mom's, is in the driveway; TV is on; Dad only watches the news on TV unless it's with Mom; the news puts Dad in a bad mood; you've learned not to ask him for money when he's in a bad mood, and so on. No going out tonight! Not unless Mom comes home soon.

So, when you hear laughter coming from the living room, it's a complete surprise. You peek around the corner, and there's your mom! She smiles in greeting, then sees your look, goes through her own set of shortcuts, to explain, 'My car's in the shop.'

Mystery solved.

A moment later your dad, going through his own set of shortcuts, says, "Grab my wallet from the other room, Kiddo. You could probably use some cash, huh? For the weekend?"

All's well that ends well.

All those shortcuts work great for quickly spitting out the daily answers to daily problems. And all those shortcuts, over the years, work very well at walling-in our thinking. We forget those interim steps. We worked them out years, even decades, even lifetimes ago for handed-down ideas, and have simply forgotten why we came to the conclusions we did, which maybe were justified then, but which may not be justified now.

Old thinking. Walled-in thinking. We get stuck in our ways. It doesn't take long. Even 20-year-olds can get stuck in their ways.

I was stuck in *my* ways. For all that fresh thinking I was so proud of, I wasn't thinking very freshly. The bell of 'absolute responsibility' was ringing in my head, and I truly could not understand why.

My mom passed away while I was in the navy. There was no warning, no indication of illness.

In port our boat had one telephone line for crew use, up forward in a room called 'control.' It was about 3 a.m. I was on watch back aft in the maneuvering room. There was a 'whoop whoop' from the ship's interior communication system. Another guy on watch with me answered it. He looked over at me. 'John, man, your *dad* is on the phone in control.'

That phone in control hardly ever rang at night. And dads don't call for no reason. Everyone knew that. Even as I was learning I had a call, someone up forward was running to wake up my watch relief, so I could take the call. When my relief arrived a couple minutes later, he just grabbed my clipboard with the watchstander's logs from me, no questions, no formal turnover. "Go, man," is all he said.

By the time I got forward, I knew. I just knew. How many reasons are there for a dad to call in the middle of the night? So, when I got the news that Mom had had a massive heart attack, and was gone…it wasn't a surprise, somehow.

Among other things—baking, braiding rugs, hanging *wallpaper*, old houses, history (anything colonial), cocktails and candlelit dinners in dark restaurants, dogs, chatting with friends at the kitchen table, drinking coffee and smoking her Pall Malls—Mom liked to knit. All the kids, for their first Christmas, got their own hand-knit Christmas stocking. I still have mine. My wife never fails to hang it up at Christmas, and every Christmas morning I never fail to find something in it, put there, no doubt, by Santa himself.

It's the little things, isn't it, that make Life great.

I got called a 'reprobate,' ironically enough, in Corpus Christi (Latin translation: 'body of Christ'), Texas, by a 'born-again' Christian.

It was late. We were alone in a science lab aboard an ocean survey vessel owned by the U.S. Environmental Protection Agency. My accuser was a smart, vivacious, lovely young woman, one of the temporary science crew. I was the onboard electronics tech, a job I took fresh out of the navy.

She wasn't smiling.

We're still friends, by the way. But I had to find a dictionary on that small vessel to determine exactly what it was that she'd called me. I knew it was bad, but, not how bad (it's pretty bad). I bring it up because LUGS, to many people in this 21st Century, is all about the 'G.' All of it. And that's what we'd been talking about. We'd spent most of that day together exploring the city, and at the end she caught me out trying to undermine her faith in that 'G.'

Young and stupid me.

Faith is like the mainsheet of a sailing vessel. It's the rope that holds the sail in place against the wind and if you break it, sail flapping in the breeze the boat loses all or much of its driving force and steering, placing it at mercy of wave and wind. The only sure way to lose a sheet, perhaps as it becomes frayed, is to have another handy, as a replacement. Had my friend's faith been frayed, had it been less than sound, the force of my arguments may have succeeded in breaking it, but where might that have left her?

Not just God, even mundane things like, say, cars: it's so easy to point out the ills. They're ridiculously expensive for the environment. Wasteful of non-renewable fuel. Take up extremely valuable urban space. They are inefficient as people movers. They turn mild-mannered citizens into speeding, road-rage prone maniacs. They don't last long. They kill people and wildlife. Their roads are expensive to build and maintain. The tires can't even be recycled.

So, are you convinced yet, to give up your car? Or do you still need it to get to work?

Problems are easy to find. They're everywhere. Solutions, however?

When we were first married, when my wife or I set the table, there was always a salt shaker on it because that's how we were taught as kids, that tables are set with salt shakers. Neither of us use salt anymore (after the cooking part is over), so over the years we've gotten to where now, if someone asks, we have to search for that table shaker of salt. Usually it's buried in the back of the crowded spice shelf, not because we put it there on purpose, but because that's where it ends up after months of not being used. But if someone wants salt, back on the table the shaker goes.

Maybe we can do that with God.

If you want salt, have some salt; if you want God, believe in God.

It's like Hildi. You can't tell me that Hildi doesn't matter. I grew up with her. To me, she does matter. To say that she's just a dog, so how could she matter, doesn't cut it. Likewise, to say God is a 'myth,' or a 'crutch,' doesn't cut it either.

It's not the 'thing'; it's the experience of the 'thing.'

Those who grew up with God, grew up with God as much as I grew up with Hildi, and usually much more. Maybe 'He' didn't push them out of bed every night, as Hildi did with little boy Johnny, but it's likely 'He' did push them, with their whole family, out of the house every weekend or so, to attend services of some nature or other, with dozens of other families from their neighborhood, and with millions of other families from around the world.

That's a powerful 'myth.'

Ask a bright, non-religious, young adult if she/he believes in the simple dictum, 'Life has meaning'—not in 'God'—just in that dictum: 'Does Life have meaning?'

It won't be easy to get a straight answer.

Many will think it's a trick question. Others simply don't want to consider it, or never have. Of the answers you might get, most will be of the non-committal variety because that dictum, 'Life has meaning,' is strongly tied to the idea of 'God.'

'Yeah, maybe'; 'I guess'; 'I don't care, because I'm my own person': those are the types of answers you'll get. They don't want to say 'no,' because of the obvious implication that then nothing has meaning; but they don't what to say 'yes,' either, because, oh no, that might involve God.

That's unfortunate.

Those of us who believe in a god have a place, be it Jesus, or Allah—whatever the deity—upon which to stand and from which to announce to the world, 'this is where I start'; 'this is where I make my stand'; 'this is my center.'

Such a center is a sturdy foundation upon which to build Life. It provides a rally point, a refuge, a place of solace and comfort. But for the rest of us? Lacking belief in any god, what place have we, but our own lonely selves? Unless we call a barricade against the belief in any god a 'foundation'—or maybe one of the 'isms' that make the rounds, humanism, existentialism, objectivism, and so on—then we have no such place.

That's what's 'unfortunate.'

So, in the interest of providing a solution, and not merely pointing out the problems...if we strip away all the trappings, the vestments, the headgear, the incantations, dogma, guilt, and sacred cows of religion, if we get right down to the idea of what God does, for those who believe, it's very simple.

God allows Life to have meaning.

Good people fail, while bad thrive: Why! Children die in their parent's arms: Why! It can seem so amorally random, and immorally evil. Without the 'guiding hand' of a god, it seems there is nothing to protect 'meaning' from being crushed by 'causation,' from one thing 'causing,' inevitably, in the vast cauldron of the universe, effects so seemingly, senselessly random, or worse, the intentional events of our fellow man.

But, if you *believe*?

If you believe, then Life becomes a picture painted by God.

While I'd never truly 'believed,' neither had I not believed. So here I was, a young man who had yet to confront himself on the issue of 'god,' and I think, looking back, for the same reason that many young people don't confront themselves on it. We don't want to abandon meaning, but 'meaning' and God, in our youthful heads, are welded, linked, short-circuited together, fused like bomb and detonator so that to mess with either, is to blow up both!

God is opaque. To believe in God is to have a reason for everything, and an explanation for nothing, because 'He' provides no explanations.

God works in mysterious ways.

And that 'mystery' does work. Like salt on the table, that's what people do—many anyway—salt their own Life, as needed, with the mystery of God. Through 'Him' they find the 'reason' they need, sans explanation, for whatever they must do. Move forward, move on, try to do the right thing, try to live a good life, a life true to themselves and to those around them. In good people, the salt of the Earth kind of people that most are, the opacity of God does not matter because ultimately the explanation does not matter, because living a life true is all that matters.

But that opacity?

It can hide people, even good people, from their own selves. It can hide motives from others. Certainly, it justifies in words, if not in fact, anything done 'in the name of God,' because opacity itself ensures that no one, often not even those proclaiming it, can see through to the 'truth,' whatever it may be, true or not.

'In the glory of God' is a great place to hide, even from oneself.

On the other hand, to be lacking in God, to remove 'Him' from the equation of Life—thus seemingly removing 'meaning' as well—is to grant free rein to causation, to the epic amorality of unchecked 'cause and effect.' And from that Big Bang-birthed juggernaut there is but one sure 'salvation,' it seems, for the conscious being: free will.

Isn't that how it works? Our free will, the free will of a conscious being, intervening in the incessant march of causation, reaching out its conscious hand to actively guide an event? But doesn't free will itself, then, lead to the amoral, the immoral, the unworthy acts of our fellow man, guiding events for their own selfish desires, in disregard of others? And what's the 'meaning' of that?

Looking back, it's clear to me that I had long ago given up any belief in any 'god,' anywhere, and simply didn't know it. I hadn't admitted it to myself. And indeed, I'd given up any belief at all in 'hidden' meaning. I had become convinced, as I still am, that everything we need to live a life true is right here. Within reach.

> *"If I ever go looking for my heart's desire again, I won't look any farther than my own back yard because if it isn't there, I never really lost it to begin with"*
> **—Dorothy, in *The Wizard of Oz* (1939)**

It was the 'lesson' Dorothy learned, and maybe it seemed like a throwaway line in the movie, but that backyard? It is the house of Life. The Life of each of us.

I didn't think of it in terms of 'house of Life,' not then I didn't. But I had come to believe, even going back to high school I'd come to believe, that there is no truth essential to living that cannot be found from within our own Life, NOW. There is no secret book, or hidden cave of lost knowledge, no treasure trove of ancient wisdom that would reveal secrets essential, *now*, to Life.

Think of it like Eden. Life provides. And those things, 'the lost wisdoms,' were they to exist, having been found they might then, perhaps, serve to guide and lead and inspire at the time they came to light. But at any given point, *now*, having not been found…they are not *needed*.

Put another way, the destination might lie far off over the horizon. But the road? It lies ever underfoot.

When I discovered 'absolute responsibility,' and I didn't realize it at the time, but the reason the bell of it rang so very, very true, and still does, is because I'd found that thing I'd thought I'd given up, when I gave up any vestige of belief in God.

Meaning.

I didn't know how it could work, I didn't know how it would work, I just knew, somehow, that 'absolute responsibility' did work. Call it my faith. A new sheet for my mainsail.

As the bell of absolute responsibility rang so very true in my head, I knew that the only entity responsible for the meaning of my Life...was me.

Which might seem selfish. 'Me' centered. But, 'particle/wave,' I am more than 'me.' I only can exist because of all the things around me that also do exist. Which makes all those things around me, the experience of all those things around me, part of me.

It's not selfish; it's all encompassing.

4

SHARED DIFFERENT WORLDS

November 2016

"I have a toy gun," the five-year-old exclaimed to his friend. "A REALLY good one!" He goes running upstairs to get the toy, and comes back a few seconds later. "Shoot me, Johnny! Shoot me!" he cries, handing the toy to his astonished friend. Me.

'Astonished,' because, one, I don't know about you, but when I was a kid playing 'army,' or whatever version of shoot 'em up we were playing, you didn't stand up against the wall and tell your buddy to shoot you. The accepted way to do it was to hide behind a piece of furniture, or a tree, or, if we were at my house, hide in a ditch next to the cornfield, and from that safe cover do your best to 'kill' the other guy. And, two, when you had a neat toy, you didn't just hand it over to the other kid. You showed it off first. You *held on to it* and showed the other kid what it could do, and then handed it over, but only after the kid was almost begging for the thing. But Tommy just handed that toy gun to me instantly—I remember it like it was yesterday—then he ran to stand up against the far wall saying, "Shoot me, Johnny! Shoot me!"

Having this nifty toy gun in my hand I thought, ok, it's his gun, if that's what Tommy wants, that's what Tommy wants. His brother Teddy (not their real names) was over in the corner playing with trucks or something, but Teddy was a lot younger than us, so pretty useless as far as we were concerned.

I remember marveling at this old toy gun of Tommy's, and how they really knew how to make toys in the old days. It was the weight of it. That's how I 'knew' it was old, because in my five-year-old brain, old toys were heavy toys (pre-plastic).

So, there I was, standing about ten feet away from Tommy as he stood up against the wall of his family's rec room, like the willing victim of a one-man firing squad (that being me), aiming the gun at him and trying to pull the trigger. But it didn't want to pull.

"There's something wrong with this thing," I told Tommy. But he just repeated, "Shoot me, Johnny. Shoot me!"

It finally occurred to me to put two hands on the gun, so now with two fingers, I squeezed as hard as I could...

BANG!

You guessed it. The real gun, fired a real bullet.

A little hole appeared in the wood paneling about three inches above the middle of Tommy's head, and grown-ups, suddenly, were everywhere.

End of fun.

It wasn't the last time I was ever in Tommy's house. A few years later I remember us kids going over to see that bullet hole. And I remember Tommy leading us upstairs to show us where he'd gotten the gun, in the drawer of his dad's bedside table (lo and behold, the gun was still there). But, it was the last time I was actually *allowed* over at Tommy's house.

I know that my dad went over that evening and some words were spoken. And Tommy and Teddy were no longer allowed to come across to our house, either. That was their parent's rule, not ours. A kind of retaliatory, 'if yours aren't allowed at ours, then ours aren't allowed at yours,' kind of thing. I remember my mom telling me it was all too bad, because it was like punishing the kids for the parents' stupidity for letting a child get hold of a loaded revolver.

There was a whole gang of us who lived on that block of Burnt Mill Road: Bill and Craig, Judy and Benji, Patty and Suzy (forgive me if I got some names wrong, it's a been a long time), and they'd all come over to play at our house. We lived across the street from 'the development,' in an old house with two friendly dogs, and a basement with a dart board and electric trains and a mysterious, unused well with a wooden cover, plus daddy long-leg spiders and other cool stuff. We had a huge yard with a barn-like garage, goats in the field behind the house, dirt pits, peat moss, vegetable patches, and an *excellent* climbing tree. We had a mom who let us all get dirty, and cleaned up the kids who weren't supposed to get dirty, especially the girls, before they went home, and best of all, who made us cookies and Jell-O and Kool-Aid and stuff. And we had a dad who tossed baseballs and footballs for us, endlessly, in a side yard big enough almost for a whole baseball field, or football, depending on the season. When the weather was good, he'd come home from work and we'd be waiting for him, the whole neighborhood, because we knew he'd toss his suit jacket aside, loosen his tie and start hitting grounders for us, or pop-ups, or whatever, without even going in the house.

But Tommy and Teddy, who lived right in the middle of it all, were no longer a part of any of it, at all, because Tommy thought his dad's gun was a toy, and I'd believed him. It didn't matter, to us, that it was a loaded gun, because that wasn't our experience of it. To us it was a toy. We treated it as a toy, and played with it as a toy.

Isn't that the way the world 'is,' for all of us, kid or not? Don't we play with the world as we see it? Is there any other way to play with the world, other than to play with it as we see it?

I think it was my wife, then girlfriend, who first introduced me to the 'Seth' books. Seth was 'channeled' by
the 'author,' Jane Roberts (in quotes because she herself
said she didn't write them). She went in a trance and
spoke 'Seth's' words as her husband wrote them down or
recorded them, but waking she claimed to have no recollection of what she'd just said. And while it has been,
now, nearly 30 years since I picked up any of the books,
it was 'Seth' who opened my mind to the idea that the
world that *is*…isn't.

Just as a little thought experiment: tomorrow, hordes
of metallic aliens invade Earth. To these aliens, lead is
like chocolate. They eat it. So they laughed, when we
shot our guns at them, because it was like shooting them
with chocolate chips. One enterprising private in the
metallic 'defense forces' took the assault rifle his desper-
ate attacker had used on him back to his home planet,
patented it as a candy launcher toy, sold it to kids, and
made a fortune—until he ran out of bullets (gunpowder
was a mystery to them). But, seriously, they thought, the
aliens did, that the strange, soft creatures of Earth were
trying to appease them with flying food. Cute little
things, humans.

Silly, sure. But the point is, that the experience of a
'gun' is relative to who or what is experiencing the gun.
Put another way, it's not the 'thing'; it's the experience
of the thing. And, especially as a youth, when everything
is new and fresh and we're still actively learning our way,
the experience we have of Life at any point, works to
shape the way we view Life from that point forward.
And, how we view Life, in turn, shapes our experience
of Life.

It's a back and forth thing. Like a mirror. When we
look in a mirror, we see ourselves. When we look at a
gun, we see not just a 'gun,' we see our feelings about

guns. And those feelings will affect how we deal with guns.

Faced with a gun, perhaps found in a drawer, if we're afraid of guns, that will affect the way we handle the gun as we pick it up, or even whether we pick it up at all. If we think it's a toy, we might casually grab it. If we're under duress, thinking there's an intruder in the house, we may find ourselves uncontrollably shaking, as we pick it up. Even if we're not under duress, but we're not familiar with guns, we may find ourselves fearful, as we pick it up, as our imagination runs riot.

The point is, in a very real way, there is no such thing as a simple 'gun.' What there is, is a thing that we can call a 'gun' but is, in fact, many different things (many different experiences) to many different people.

A gun can be a toy, a symbol of repression, or of victory, a metaphor for war, or peace. A gun found in a nightstand might mean, for its owner, a distrust of the neighbors, or of a whole society; it can mean a fear of criminals, or fear of government; it can represent safety and well-being; it can be an expression of masculinity, or bravado. It might symbolize a feeling of inadequacy. It might be an expression of solidarity with the Second Amendment of the U.S. Constitution, the right to bear arms.

It might 'mean' any number of things, to any number of people. And that meaning will affect not just how we view guns intellectually, but how we actually handle them, and treat them, or even if we handle them at all.

When we look in a mirror, we see ourselves. When we look at a gun, we're also seeing ourselves, in the sense that we're seeing our take on guns.

And not just guns. Everything. The husband sees his expensive, ratcheting, 13mm combination wrench on the floor of the garage. The wife sees grease on a shiny tool-thingy on the floor of the garage. The wife sees backward letters on their child's homework, and wonders if he might be dyslexic. The husband sees the 'C' marked on the top, and tells the kid to 'work harder.'

We see different worlds. We see our world relative to us, to who we are. And how we see our world is a reflection of who we are, to the point that in a very real way, we see, in looking at our world, a mirror of ourselves. How we see our world, how we react to our world, is, ultimately, a reflection of who we are.

It's called, lamely, 'relative reality.' It's the notion that the world is not an absolute, one-size-fits-all place, but instead is relative, in effect, to the observer (like the speed of light, if in an off-hand way).

It's a weird way of looking at it, sure. It's a perspective thing. But if we look at Life as an experience, then, if the experience is different, might it make sense that Life is different?

Looking back, at the time, what the notion of 'relative reality' did for me more than anything was get me to re-evaluate my relationship with my world. Indeed, it became 'my world.' No longer was 'the world' an absolute that existed independently of me. Now there was a give and take between 'us.' Between the world and me, indeed, between everything and me.

And there are all kinds of implications to this relative way of looking at the world. No longer was I bouncing against a world that was. Period. Instead, I was interacting. And maybe that's merely a change in perspective, but it is a powerful change, nonetheless. Before, if I wanted to change the world, I had to chip at it, bang my head against it, rail at it. It was so big! I mean, you know, you live here too.

But with a 'relative' world, a world that changes with you, then change is not an 'out there' thing. It's an 'in here' thing. As I change, so does the world. I'm the one controlling the story. Indeed, I'm the one deciding what has changed in the world, relative to me, because it is *my* story. I'm the one deciding what is, and what isn't, important to me, part of my story. So, no longer do I bounce against a world 'that is what it is,' irrespective of me. Instead, I interact with a world that responds to me, changing with me as I change with it, back and forth, like a communication we respond to each other.

Like a communication.

Like a relationship.

And again, it can seem so silly: change the world by changing me? It seems childish. But—big but—what the world is, to you, is up to you. You're the one looking at it. You're the one interacting with it. You're the one responding to it. Your world, is yours alone. You're the one building the story of you.

That's not silly.

There is another implication of relative reality. And that is, that you and I, and it's a little bit weird to say it this way, but you and I share different worlds.

We live in different worlds, but we share our different worlds as well, sharing with each other what we have in common with our worlds. More than that, we communicate, not necessarily directly, but with the people we know. Talking with each other, sharing our experiences and our world with each other. Much of youth is all about validating individual experience, comparing notes, so to speak, on experiences, establishing a kind of baseline of shared experience, individually and culturally.

Yes, we share different worlds, but we share each other as well, the commonalities we all have that make us human, that make us mammal, that make us alive and living on Earth.

Look at all the great kinetic whirl of our universe, billions of galaxies, each with billions of stars, over billions of years, and you and I and all of us, sharing the same (99.9% the same) DNA, here, now, together on the same planet at the same time—in a cosmic sense, no kidding, we are all but identical. *Identical.* So, is it any wonder that our individual worlds look so much alike that we mistake them for being exactly the same worlds?

Weird way of looking at it?

My dad loved to fly. He got his private pilot license, earning the money by fixing televisions, shortly after graduating from West Catholic High School in Philadelphia. Years later, when he became the Midwest sales rep for an electronics manufacturing firm, Dad made use of that pilot's license and bought an airplane, using it to fly around to clients, writing it off as a business expense. Handy!

For Thanksgiving one year, he and Mom loaded the three kids in the rear seat of that single-engine Mooney, tight squeeze, and flew the family across Lake Michigan all the way to a little airport near my grandmother's house. Alas, the weather closed in over the weekend, and my dad didn't have an instrument rating (no flying through clouds). Arrangements were made to take a commercial flight home, and a friend was contacted to pick us up after we landed.

We got to the airport departure gate in plenty of time, and seeing that there was an earlier flight that hadn't yet left, my dad, the business traveler, knowing his way around airports as he did, hustled us down to 'standby' hoping to catch that earlier flight. But it was post-Thanksgiving; all seats were booked, and he wasn't the only one who knew about standby. We found ourselves last in a longish line.

I remember it was well-lit, cold and kind of dingy downstairs where we waited. There were no seats so we had to stand, impatiently leaning against a wall. My mom knelt down to explain to her three boys what was going on, to just be patient, and not to get our hopes up. But only moments after explaining this, she hurriedly gathered us up and hustled us to the front of the line, past swiveling heads and complaining voices. Through an

outside door into the cold November air we went,
straight up the stairs onto the plane! Hurray! We'd made
it!

It seems there were exactly five empty seats, and the
only way to fill each valuable one and keep all interested
parties together on the same plane, was to seat the party
of five. We were on!

A few hours later, having landed, my dad called his pal
to let him know we'd arrived. Much to his surprise the
man, a grizzled Korean War vet, broke down in tears
right there on the phone. He'd been watching the news,
and he knew our flight number, and our flight, the flight
we'd originally been booked on, shortly after take-off, it
had crashed.

He'd thought we were all dead.

'Fate'? 'Luck'? 'Karma'? 'Divine intervention'? Pick a
'reason.' But in terms of bald 'cause and effect,' it's a
pretty straightforward story.

Indeed, the story itself is told in 'cause and effect'
terms, and is nicely wrapped up, beginning, middle, and
end, just like all good stories should be. And that's a big
reason why causation can be made to work as an explanation, for anything, at all. Because it's the tellers of the
tale who get to choose the starting points, the ending
points, the important points, and indeed, the characters.

When a portion of the ever-changing universe gets
walled off into a 'story,' it turns the normally open system
of the universe—the cause and effect relationship between all 'things' going back to whenever all things became 'all' things—into a more-or-less strictly but artificially defined closed system, a system of severely limited
boundaries, and selected parts.

A large part of being human is interpreting the events
of Life. And in that story of our Life, we choose the
boundaries of the story, we choose the major characters,
and the minor, we choose what's important, and what's
not.

It's our Life, after all.

'People died in our place.' That's an angle on the story that wasn't taken, but could have been. Because if we hadn't shown up at the back of the line, some of those people in the front of the line might not have been on the plane that went down.

There is also the 'overworked dad' version. The reason we had to rush to find a flight that day, besides having to be at school on Monday, was so Dad could make a meeting at work. Should that have been part of the story?

Was it a rash decision in the first place, made on the part of both parents, to fly off for a quick visit to grandma with no built-in buffer for travel delays, in a small plane, during a holiday, with winter approaching? Should that be part of the story?

Do we even know all the facts of the story? Maybe the employee in charge of boarding took pity on a stressed mom having to shepherd three tired boys and luggage all over the airport. Maybe she/he just made up the part about 'exactly five seats' to quell the discontent of the adults ahead of that family.

Maybe there were six empty seats, and not five, but in the rush and hurry of boarding there was a miscount. Again, not part of the story, but we don't know the entire story, so we can only construct our story from the pieces we have.

What happened to the ticket holders of those empty seats? Was someone running headlong with their bags through the airport to make that plane, even as we were being ushered onto the plane?

Was there, maybe, a family of three, perhaps with a four-year-old loudly complaining of hunger, that showed up at 'standby' before our family of five, but upon seeing the line, gave up to get the kid something to eat?

Ultimately, we don't know the entire story. We can't know the entire story. We can only work off what we know, or were told, or speculate, or think we know, or squeeze in to make it work, or make up as we go along, then build a wall around the parts of the story that seem most appropriate (risky decision, out; overworked dad, out; number of empty seats, in; a dad who knew his way around airports, in) construct a story, and build the arc of our lives from there.

And then, of course, there are all the potential 'if not fors.' If not for a dad who knew his way around airports, we'd all be dead. If not for a mom who had all the kids packed and ready to go early, we'd all be dead. If not for a grandad who knew his way to the airport, and dropped us off without delay, we'd all be dead. If not for five people who didn't show up at the airport, we'd all be dead. If not for a string of party of twos or fours in front of us, we'd all be dead.

Do we focus on only one of the many 'if not fors'? So, for example, does Dad become the hero of the story because he knew his way around airports? Or are all the 'if not fors' important? Or none of them? Is there a lesson we should take from the story? 'Don't give up your place in a line'? 'Bring snacks for young children'? 'Be early for airport departures'? 'God looks out for those who know airline procedures'? Anything?

Is there a 'meaning'? Were we blessed? Were we lucky? Was someone looking out for us?

All of which might be moot, perhaps, 'if not for' the family friend who watched the news that evening, and who knew what flight we were on. Because if he hadn't watched the news, maybe there wouldn't be a 'story' in the first place, because none of us would have known how close we came to boarding a 'doomed' flight.

How many deadly accidents dodged, deadly car wrecks avoided, deadly viruses not caught, deadly fires not started, deadly anythings, have all of us 'missed' over the years of our collective lives? Good news! If we're alive, all of them!

Which brings up, maybe, a less than obvious question, but, would that next flight have been 'doomed' if my family had gotten on it? Is there any way to know? Because with different people boarding, in a different order, might other factors have come into play? Little things can add to big things, and Life is not built of large events alone anyway. Maybe it would have taken nothing more than a pilot finding himself with a few extra seconds that he otherwise wouldn't have had, and seeing, for instance, a worrying anomaly in a fuel pressure reading, or, calling for a weather update, and learning that a developing thunderstorm had just been reported on the intended flight path.

Perversely, if that scenario is deemed plausible, that maybe that plane wouldn't have crashed if we'd been aboard, then it might seem that the 'cause' of the crash was my family of five *not* boarding!

Silly? Sure. But plausible? Absolutely, depending on your point of view. Because stories can be shaped, twisted, interpreted, almost any way at all.

Which might all seem perfectly innocent. It's just a 'story,' after all...

The missed flight story is all about looking backward at Life. In one sense, in real time, that story didn't even happen. We already hadn't been in a plane crash, when we realized we hadn't been in a plane crash. It is only by looking 'backward' at it, that it becomes a story.

In a sense, causation is itself *only* about looking backward. It can always be made to 'work'—we can always find an 'explanation,' even if only for ourselves—when looking backward. Thing A 'caused' thing B, which is 'why' events resulted in outcome Z. But, looking forward? Can anyone predict the future?

Even scientific experiments, tightly walled and rigorously controlled, no matter whether they go right or wrong, while they can be used to 'predict' the 'future' within tightly walled parameters, they can't predict every last detail—whatever did happen to Schrödinger's cat?

Life imposes itself.

And when it comes to Life itself, not the walled-off life of experiments, but real Life, the Life of you and me?

We can't wall in the future. We can't construct boundaries for our predicted 'story.' The future doesn't recognize boundaries. Within the ever-changing drama of Life, everything comes into play. Every atom, every electron, if they exist as a 'cause,' they generate an 'effect.' They all play a role. They can all affect an outcome.

And even in real time, even right NOW, this instant, do we always know how we ended up 'here,' NOW? Or are we more likely to be able to make sense of things at some point when NOW has turned into 'then,' and we find ourselves looking backward at where we used to be (and maybe still are), but with time to 'construct' a 'story'?

No two 'stories,' even of the same event, are the same. Is it any wonder?

There is an assumption that the world 'is' a certain way, and that while, yes, we may construct 'stories' about Life, those stories don't alter the true facts of the case. That airliner *did* crash, as an example; we *were* booked on it, but we *weren't* actually on it. End of story, because the facts of the world, are the facts of the world.

And yes, looking backward there are indeed lots of 'facts,' some of them indeed indisputable. But does that make the past, indisputably, 'THE PAST'? Or do the 'facts' we know of the past merely set the stage, so to speak, for a drama that is still playing, in our head, as we ponder Life? Have you never had the experience of real-izing, now, that what happened 'then,' didn't happen the way you thought it had? An, 'oh, *that's* what she meant!'; '*that's* why she did that!'; '*that's* what happened!' kind of moment?

"'I see!' said the blind carpenter, as he picked up his hammer, and saw." (My dad used to say that, a lot, too.)

To re-imagine the past, is to change our story of who we are, how we got here, and so on. And that story of who we are, individually, is the basis upon which we build our responses to Life going forward.

Contrast the past—the 'thing A caused thing B resulting in outcome Z,' causational basis upon which we build the stories of our past—with the 'future.' Looking forward there is no 'causation'; there are no 'stories.' What there is, is prediction, expectation, extrapolation, calculation, speculation, etc., all based, ultimately, on the 'cause and effect' lessons we have learned by looking backward at our lives, lessons learned from our 'story' of our past. But are there facts?

Are there any 'facts,' at all, over the horizon of NOW? Is anything 'set in stone,' forever?

The stories we build of our 'past,' and the expectations we hold of our 'future,' all 'exist' in our NOW. And NOW, our feeling of the moment that is right NOW, is the only 'place' past and future 'exist.'

The past has no existence except as it is recorded in the present
—John Archibald Wheeler (1911–2008)

We got married on a friend's backyard deck, on a bluff overlooking Mare Island Strait. My wife did everything. I flew in, showed up, said, "I do." It was pretty great.

It was a small wedding, very simple, very Californian. Everyone had a good time, even my judgmental (read, 'scary'), East Coast, Catholic aunt (my dad's sister, who surprised us with her RSVP). She was my favorite aunt, actually, of a lot of aunts (Dad was second to last of nine Irish kids). This same aunt, after her first husband had passed away, traveled to Iran, alone, before the Iranian Revolution but still, alone. She loved crafts, and she'd wanted to see the rugs! Many years later, now in her 90s and having outlived two husbands, she remarked to my wife in passing (literally, in passing, because my wife was walking past her with a tray of food in her hands) that maybe her second husband was penance for the way she'd treated her first husband.

We build our own story, each of us.

The morning after the wedding, the two happy newlyweds (and two *not*-happy cats) squeezed into a '73 Volkswagen Beetle loaded with all the bride's stuff, and began a cross-country drive to South Florida. We moved into Dad's old trailer—he moved out and we rented it from him—in a big trailer park in Margate.

I knew the park well. We'd wired every lot for cable.

5

THE WAVE VIEW

November 2016

The human body has some amazing capabilities. For example, it can detect things that happen in *atoms*.

It kind of boggles the mind to think of it that way, but that's what the eye does, detect photons. And that's where photons come from, atoms. And, according to some researchers, even a single photon can be detected by the eye.

The human eye can detect atomic level events, like a single photon—emitted by a single *atom*.

Our brains tend to interpret the world in terms of 'objects'—in terms of 'things.' That's our 'story,' a universe 'made' of 'things.' Simple.

Ocean waves, as an example, are 'made' of seawater, and seawater is 'made' of water molecules, which are 'made' of atoms, and so on, one water molecule bonded to another water molecule, with some salt and seaweed and other stuff thrown in. What else could ocean waves be 'made' of?

That very question exposes the underhanded extent of the problem. It exposes our prejudice, our ingrained belief, that the world is 'made' of 'things.'

If it's not 'made' of particles, or objects, or things, what is a wave made of?

Relationships.

So, you're at the stadium watching your favorite team do its thing. Suddenly everyone around you is standing, so you stand! Now everyone around you is sitting, so you sit!

A wave!

It marches its way around the stadium, and eventually dies. Gone. But. What. Is. It?

Is it people? There are people all over the place, but now there is no wave. It's gone. So, no, the wave is not 'made' of people.

It's 'made' of the relationship between the relative heights of people.

At the moment, with no discernable pattern of relationships between the heights of people standing and sitting in the stands, there is no 'wave.' But, when the next wave starts, there will be a discernable, and changing, pattern of relationships, sitting, standing, and even in-between.

Life is a relationship. The very words in this sentence in one sense form a 'wave,' a continually changing pattern of relationships. On its own, a letter usually communicates little or nothing...

'P.'

In context, in relation to the other letters, every letter is meaningful. They form 'p'atterns.

But even then, the word 'pattern,' by itself, may well be meaningless. It's the use of 'pattern' in a sentence, in a paragraph, in a context of ideas, that form the 'wave.' A pattern of relationships, constantly changing as our eyes scan the written words.

But still, it might seem silly. Because even pieces put together must be put together in a certain way, so as to form the things of which they are the pieces. And that's what I'm trying to show. It's not just pieces, it's relationships. To have a 'thing' of pieces those pieces must exist in a certain distinct relationship (left leg bone connected to left side of hip bone), or that 'thing' is a different thing (left leg bone connected to right side of hip bone?). All of which is a roundabout way of saying that all the various relationships between things are just as important a 'part' of the thing as the pieces themselves. Things are built of pieces *and* the relationship between them.

Put still another way, things are built of *relationships*—between pieces. (Just because we can't put our finger on it, doesn't mean it's not there; just because we can put our finger on it, doesn't mean that's the whole story.)

It's the 'wave' perspective. And to some (not-so-small) degree, the entire point of this book is to seed in you an understanding of that 'wave' perspective. (Or at least an acknowledgment that there is a 'wave perspective'!)

A slow learner, I truly am. Late bloomer too. As a youth I muddled through, somehow, saying and doing more or less the right thing, more or less most of the time. But did I know what I was doing?

No.

All those years working for my dad, working my way up to foreman of one of Dad's crews (sure, boss's son). Six years in the navy, too, but muddling all the while. Not that I wasn't conscientious (one of Dad's favorite words). That's not it. Dad never complained about my work, and neither did the navy; they sent me to a leadership school, and appointed me (surprise!) leading petty officer of E-Division (same pay, more headaches—welcome to the real world). But still, I was muddling. I was doing it because it was my job; because it was expected of me; because as I looked at it, the work I did reflected on me, and I cared what others thought of me. Which, on one hand, might seem laudable—the boy did good work. But on the other hand, 'the boy' did good work for entirely selfish reasons. It was all about *me*.

Hardly 'laudable,' that...

One day my boss showed me the telephone room of the company we worked for. Medium-size company. Medium-size telephone room. Pre-digital, so there were

wires everywhere, all over those walls, all arrayed in perfect, color-coded order: white red black yellow violet:
blue orange green brown slate. Telephone cable color
code.

I've had four epiphanies in my life, moments of conscious perception that something—something meaningful—had filtered through all the armor and baggage and
confusions of existence, granting me a deeper, or at least
a different, understanding. This one, as mundane as it
seems, was epiphany number two. I was in my twenties.

Every wire meant something. Every wire went somewhere. Every wire was *connected*. Purposely, painstak-
ingly, perfectly, connected.

And then there was all that *work*.

He had to take a phone call, my boss, and I was left
there, in that room. Those neurons of mine, they saw
that exquisitely organized mayhem of wires and connections, and started *firing*, like waking up, and slowly my
mouth dropped open.

I kind of haven't been able to close it, properly, ever
since.

If you're not in awe of the communication systems of
our world; if you're not in awe of the power systems of
our world, and the waterworks of our world; if you're
not in awe of the constructions of our world—the free-
ways, the cities, the subways, the social networks and
computers, the cars, clothes, comfy beds, the central heat
and air-conditioning of our world, the *food* of our world
(and the coffee!), available year 'round—and if you're
not in awe of those who invent, engineer, construct, and
maintain these systems, even the ordinary efforts that it
takes to make those things work, every last day, every
last *minute*...

If you are not in awe...

The ramifications of that little telephone room visit
have shaped my world ever since—we each build our
own story. Like I say, I was always conscientious, but

ever since that day I have become more dutiful in performing my job, any job, anything I might do upon which others depend, because others do depend on it. No longer is a job something I want to get done because it looks good on me. Now, I want to get it done because it needs to be done, and it's on me to get it done. And the reason for that simple change comes down to one simple thing: Respect.

Respect for who we are; respect for *humanity*.

Yes, we do have a long, long way to go. But, humanity? My goodness, and it's not a gee-whiz thing either. It's a how much work thing, deliberate, focused, connected work. And if all of us are not privy to the wonders of that labor—if all of us can't all enjoy the comforts and conveniences and entertainments of our world—whether due to its price, our color or social status, which side of a political line in the sand we were born on, whatever—whatever might be stopping us from sharing in those wonders—that's a serious problem, for all humans.

But, please, let's not make it a condemnation, of all humanity.

Most of us, and that's most all of us, who build those things, who care for those things, who put a life's work into those things—in any capacity, right on down to the clean-up crew—we don't do it to keep others from having it; we do it so others *can* have it.

Unless, of course, we do it just for the money. Which is exactly what many of us think. It's tough not to think in terms of 'me me me' money or career, compensation of some nature or other, in this world we've created. But those many of us who think solely in terms of 'what do I get out of it,' we might ask ourselves what an ancient hunter might have been thinking, when he gave up his catch, freely, to his tribe. Money? Quid pro quo? The chief's virgin daughter? I scratch your back, you scratch mine? Is that why he gave up his catch?

Possibly.

Or, maybe—just a thought—maybe he was thinking that being able to eat well allowed the whole tribe to thrive, and, hey, he too was part of the tribe.

That's my take on it, that that's where it started. Specialized labor: it wasn't an 'I'll do it, in return for...,' kind of thing. It was an 'I'll do it, because I'm part of this thing,' kind of thing. It's pure self-interest on the part of an individual who identifies him or herself as part of a wider whole, so the well-being of the whole ensures the well-being of the self.

It's really not complicated. It wasn't a quid pro quo that spawned the idea of specialized labor. A kidney is specialized. Does it engage in labor negotiations with the heart, or brain, or gut? Does the brain seek ways to maximize production out of the heart cells, while skimming some oxygen 'pay' from those same cells, to use for itself, because it 'deserves' it, because it's the 'brains' of the operation, because it can?

When you look at a body, and you see otherwise perfectly 'able' cells taking more than their fair share, while themselves providing no service, producing nothing of value, what do you call it?

Cancer.

Ever noticed those signs, you see them on the back of trucks going down the freeway, that say, "Tired of tarping?" And then there's a phone number? They're directed at flatbed truckers.

Flatbedding is a particular kind of job for a trucker. Your load is out in the open. Anyone can see it, including the highway patrol. You have to strap it or chain it to keep it on your deck. There are a host of regulations involving that, and a host of different kinds of loads you might carry, many of which will have load-specific tiedown requirements and peculiarities.

And, a lot of loads, you have to keep it dry, and that's where tarps come in.

Tarps are big. They're heavy. They're dirty. They can be very unwieldy, especially in a gusty wind. Full size tarps can blow clean off a load, usually while the driver is in the process of draping it, standing or crawling around on top of a load of maybe wallboard, or dry lumber, stacked as high as eight feet, or more, off a deck already five feet off the ground. (Drape the upwind side first, driver, that be the trick, and the wind itself will hold it to your load.)

Everyone hates to tarp.

So why, we have to ask ourselves, and I've noticed this again and again, that without fail, when the wind is up and the rain is coming down—and in fact, the worse the conditions are, the more I've noticed it—flatbedders tarping their loads are *happy* (when there are more than one of them around).

Why?

It's enlighteningly simple. They're all of them wet. If it's winter they're all of them cold. And all of them (or most, anyway) are smiling and bantering, calling back and forth at each other, black guys, white guys, Hispanic guys, lady flatbedders, road-dog truckers, baby truckers, young or old, it doesn't matter, the more trucks are around, in close vicinity, the happier the whole crew is.

I'm not lying.

Why?

Because they are helping.

It's really simple. And doesn't that say something—something really encouraging—about humanity? A little bit of help goes a long way when tarping in a breeze of wind. And all of them are helping each other do it. Guys who wouldn't say boo to each other on a hot, dry, dusty Monday, strapping each to their own truck, on Tuesday, when the wind comes up (it's the wind that does it, rain alone the flatbedder can handle, if not happily!) they're grabbing each other's straps and tarps to hold them down and keep them from blowing off in the wind, until the other guy can secure them.

Humans, any human possessing even a scintilla of emotional health, if there is a shared goal and we're in a position where we can help, and we know our help will be appreciated, then, we *want* to help. We *like* to help.

It makes us happy to help.

Ever noticed that? That people are happy when they're helping?

Even in an office, on that day when everything goes awry, maybe when the power goes out, or all manner of unscheduled baloney hits the fan all at once, and it's not really anyone's fault, maybe, but now there is all this stuff that just *has* to get done? On those days, have you noticed, how after everyone gets over the initial shock, and the anger recedes, and the recriminations stop, and people just start putting their back to it, churning out the work...have you ever noticed (and the worse it is, the more you'll notice it), how the team jells together, helping each other, and people start to get happy?

How many mayors, of how many towns, when the reporter's microphones are put into their faces to get that 'reaction' take after a catastrophe of some nature or other has passed, when the tornadoes leave, or floodwaters are starting to recede, whatever it may be, how many of those good mayors *don't* say, "These people, in this town, these are *good* people. These are the kind of people who come together when the chips are down, and it's just so heartening to see it, everyone coming together, because these folk hereabout, they're the kind you can count on." How many of them don't say that, or some version of that? Any of them?

No.

It's not special to this town, or that, or this state, or that, or this country or that. It's special to *humans*.

Humans like to help. It makes us happy to help reach a shared goal.

And the funny thing about that, is that those of us who think in terms of compensation, when the only reason we're doing what we're doing is to get paid, so that it's just a purely selfish thing—it's not 'helping,' then. It's 'working.' And working doesn't necessarily make anyone happy. In fact, it makes a lot of us flat unhappy, especially if we feel like we're not getting paid enough, and how many of us feel, ever, that we're getting paid enough?

Heaven is like that. Isn't it? Kind of a quid pro quo? Do the right thing, now, keep it up your whole life, and you'll get paid. A trip to heaven: it's a paycheck for a life's 'work.'

Life becomes a job.

So, that little trip to the telephone room, for me? It just makes the everyday living of life all that much easier, and happier to deal with—for me it does. I don't do it anymore just to get paid (I still like to get paid —I'm not a complete idiot—but that's not the sole reason). I do it because it needs to be done. I'm *helping*. Does that sound stupid? My specialized labor is helping somebody, somewhere, do something. And I trust that the help I am providing at some level, somehow, somewhere, is appreciated.

It's helpful, of course, that I have a job that society has an honest use for. And there's a trust thing too, that my 'help' is being used honestly.

Yes, you can call it stupid, or naive if you like. Simplistic. Unrealistic. 'Delusional' might be a good description. And we could go on and on about it, about the right and wrong of who we are as a *species*, because if you don't like where it seems, to you, that our world is going, then it can sure seem stupid to be part of helping us get there.

'They paved paradise; And put up a parking lot.' Joni Mitchell sang it, and you won't get any argument from me about the plethora of boneheaded directions humanity has, over the years, pulled itself into. But that song has it wrong, because 'they' didn't put up anything; *we* did. Humans did. All of us did it, together.

It's the 'wave view' (or part of it anyway). Life is a metaphor of itself. We are each a detected human in a wave of humanity. We're all in this together. Whether we like it or not we're all in this together. And together, as a species, we can *only* go where, together, we take ourselves. If we tear ourselves apart getting there? Then 'torn' is the species that together we will be.

Ultimately, it's a trust thing; it's believing in your fellow human, because they are human, just like you. It's believing in all of humanity, indeed in all of Life, because Life gave birth to humanity. Mistakes can and will be made, and again and again, because living is a learning process. Just like individuals, species too can learn, and adapt, and evolve. So, it's a trust that we will learn. But most of all it's a trust that most of us—not all, but most of us—wrong-headed or not, we're being the best humans we can be under the entirety of circumstances in which we find ourselves.

Stupid? Naive? Delusional? Your call on that. But maybe someday, as I go about my trucking duties out there in the world, we'll meet, and talk maybe a little bit, and then I'll go off to do my thing (I'm not much for banter, too much to do!), and my departing words to you will be, 'Have fun!'

I say it all the time, and I truly do mean it. It's not a joke; it's an honest request. Most people, I don't think they get it. But, take a trip, someday, into an old-school telephone room, or maybe just look around this world of ours with a fresh set of eyes, unblinkered by any need for compensation and, who knows, maybe you will...

Have fun!

Imagine an object that lives all by itself in an infinite universe. Lonely existence. Call it a 'unit-particle,' a particle composed of nothing but itself, existing in a universe composed of that unit-particle, and nothing else besides.

So this 'unit-particle,' how 'big' is it? It's not that it matters one way or the other. That's not the point. The point is, is there a way, any way at all, for us to measure this unit-particle, to determine how 'big' it is? Because wouldn't we need some other object of known length against which to measure it, before we could know how long, or wide, or deep? Lacking any such object, is there a way to 'know' how 'big' our unit-particle is?

Similar question, but how about motion? Is our unit-particle moving? Can we know? What is it moving in relation to, to call it moving?

Does this particle have a 'charge'? Can we know? There are no other objects in this universe to generate an electrical potential between them, so, how could we know?

And mass? Does it have any? How do we know? There is nothing to pull or push it. No force can be exerted on it. Nothing to be attracted to it by gravity.

But, maybe you're thinking that this unit-particle might have all kinds of qualities, but because there is only the unit-particle in this universe, it's simply a case of not being able to *experience* those qualities; it doesn't mean it doesn't have those qualities. Just because your mom, for example, never showed you the birthmark she had on her rear-end, so you never were able to 'experience' the birthmark—not that you wanted to—that doesn't mean that she didn't have the birthmark.

Certainly, just because you haven't seen it, doesn't mean it's not there. But if *no one* has seen it? Including your mom? Including anyone or anything at all? Does 'it' 'exist' then?

Put another way, if you, or anyone or anything, has no experience of a cat on your lap, is there a cat on your lap?

If there is no experience of a thing, *at all*, does it exist? Can it exist?

Can a 'thing' of no experiential qualities, of no qualities that can be experienced, with no relationship to any other 'thing,' exist at all?

That's the point. To exist, there must be experience of it. And that experience implies a relationship.

We're singing the song. Can you hear it? The relations between the 'notes,' particle, wave, energy, length? Off key a little here and there, maybe, but still, singing. Pointing out that the qualities of an individual object, exist as a relationship between different objects.

Objects, on their own, lacking that 'relationship' (like removing the relationship between 'attern' and 'p'), don't have qualities.

Relationships grant qualities. Particle/wave.

Can you hear it!

Wave: the relation between units. Particle: a single unit.

The relationship, the wave, doesn't exist without the detected particles; the particles don't exist as part of that wave, without the wave of relationships between them.

> *...the more we have studied it, the less the world seems comprehensible in terms of something that is. It seems to be a lot more intelligible in terms of relations between events*
> **—Carlo Rovelli *The Order of Time* (Riverhead Books, 2018)**

We didn't last long in South Florida. It wasn't a good fit with my new wife. Bugs were high on her list (palmetto bugs darting under bathroom cabinets when the light came on, that kind of stuff), but it was more than that. South Florida is...it's the U.S. deep South, but with coconuts and a New York accent, so, yeah, kind of unexplainable.

After about six months (we were at an upscale shopping mall in Boca Raton, and she looked around, West Coast gal that she is, and said, 'There's no black people here'; that's when I caved), I suggested we move back to

California. She jumped at the idea. She had her old job back the next day, and with one of the two cats and my brother as company, drove out the next week in her VW bug and got us an apartment in Oakland. I followed a couple months later, after getting untied from work, with the rest of our gear and the other cat.

And nine months later, almost to the day, after I and that cat moseyed into our beautiful new digs on Perkins Street, Life had a new person to love.

6

INFINITY

January 2017

We were living in Oakland when it happened, at our place off 9th Avenue.

I was writing a novel. I'd been laid off from my job as a shipyard electrician, so with the blessing of my wife I took a year off to do it. The idea was to convey my thoughts in a fictional format. The setting, the story, the characters and how they responded and how they thought, all that would kind of embody the ideas I had. That was my thinking. And I could make some money to boot, and have a career. Great idea, huh?

And I threw in some pithy sayings as well, things like, 'being your world, is what you are.' Which maybe gives you an idea why...put it this way, you don't grow used to rejection letters, you grow allergic to them.

My 'office' in our aging, rented townhouse opened from a set of French doors off the master bedroom on the second floor. The window by my desk opened onto a maple tree, which served as the main doorway into and out of the house for the cats. Up the tree, across the branch, short leap onto the window sill, and then onto my lap.

It was there that I wrote the fiction. And one day, leaning back in my chair, staring into space contemplating…who knows what, computer on the desk in front of me, maple tree through the window to the left…

I don't know what to call it. A vision? An upgrade?

I've come to believe in, well, maybe we could call it 'serendipity.' It's kind of like 'providence,' at least in my mind, but without the divine part. Leave God out of providence, and you have serendipity.

In a way, to believe in yourself, to believe that you are on the right path, to believe, even, that it's possible to break the boundaries that hold you back, and forge yourself anew, you *have* to believe in serendipity. Because we can't 'see' all. We can't 'know' all. We can't consciously be all that we are. So, as I see it, we have to believe that the road we are on, is the road that takes us to where we need to be, each of us individually. Faith: It's a real thing. And shakers of salt need not be involved.

Even if things go terribly, terribly wrong, it is serendipity, wielding its hammer, forging us, each of us, each of us *forging ourselves*, because some things, sometimes, just have to be learned the hard way. That's Life. There are some things too, that can't be hurried. It's like a cake; we have to wait for it to bake, and it can take so, *so* interminably long.

And there are indeed some places, it's very true, that to get there, we kind of have to already be there. Maybe that's where death comes in, and birth. Because Life is not material alone, not merely ashes to ashes, dust to dust particles; Life exists as 'wave' as well, as that relationship between 'things,' that differentiates 'things.' Life is experience *never-ending*, not an object, inevitably failing…

I don't know how long it lasted. Twenty minutes? Forty? A lifetime? Possibly.

And there is no way to describe it. Branches of trees, never-ending. It wasn't a vision, but it was. It wasn't anything, but it was. So how do you describe that?

It really was like an upgrade, like a registry entry attached to every file: 'Infinity.' But it's one thing to write about it. It's another thing to *live* it, *see* it, *be* it.

Not that I'm infinite and you're not. We're all infinite. But it's that wave thing. It's a way of looking at things that doesn't only see 'things,' that loses that boundary between one 'thing' and another. Infinity is the infinity of things, but infinity doesn't end. And things...things don't exist of themselves, for all things are collections of other things. But the collections never end. Smaller or larger, no end to the collections. And 'smaller' and 'larger' don't really exist either, because there is no smaller or larger, because in infinity all things are the same 'size': infinite.

Scale is a dimension of the infinite. Scale, in three dimensions, is a dimension of infinite spacetime. (I did mention the vision, right?)

And when that vision of the infinite, when it doesn't end, when there is no 'smallest part,' no end to the things of which other things are made, so things, in the end, become made of things that have no 'end.' And when, in the other direction, there is no end to the collection of things, when every collection of things is part of another collection of things, never-ending, when there is no 'biggest,' no final collection that IS, something...

When there is no final collection of pieces being something, *there is no* 'something.'

What do you have, if you have no something? You have no thing. You have nothing.

Infinity and zero feed each other.

But 'nothing,' never-ending? There *is no* universe of 'nothing.' 'Nothing' only exists in relation to something. It's meaningless to say, for example, that you have no nothing. But it is perfectly meaningful to say that you have no cat on your lap.

Zero devolves into the infinite. The infinite evolves into zero.

Yin and Yang?

It's not a new idea. But when it engulfs you—and it's not like you wake up with a halo around your head either. Nothing really changes. Until…

It was night, somewhere south of Corning, on the southbound side of Interstate-5 in Northern California, when three words came to me. Twenty-five years, or so, since that infinity vision, and it was like having another vision, but now with no maple tree out the window on my left, and of course my eyes were open too. I was driving, an '06, W900 Kenworth tractor—an honest 500 horsepower, and maybe 1,900 foot-pounds of torque, dialed into an ISX Cummins diesel, mated to a mountain-flattening, 13-speed, Eaton-Fuller transmission, *sweet* ride—pulling roofing, or maybe lumber, strapped to an old, steel, flatbed trailer.

'Awareness.'

'Creation.'

'Life.'

The road was long, and smooth. The huge, straight, white hood of that Kenworth loomed out in front of me, gleaming amber from the reflection of the clearance lamps on the roofline above the windshield.

The relationships that exist between all the 'particles' of Life, that is 'awareness,' a metaphor in a sense for the changing pattern of relationships, in another sense, for the infinity of 'no things.'

What we 'build,' that is 'creation,' a metaphor in one sense for the 'particles' of the world, the infinity of 'things.'

Without one, there is no other. With one, there is always the other.

'Life' is the amalgamation of the two, becoming one. It is the coin of two sides: heads, awareness; tails, creation.

Awareness/creation: Life.

Tails/heads: coin.
Zero/infinity: universe.
Mom/dad: Me.
Life is a metaphor of itself. It really is.

The books never sold. My wife had a career. I didn't.
I was a stay-at-home dad, but lacking a steady stream of
new kids, that's not a long-term career.

At a get-together one day I found two friends, drinks
in hand, discussing LUGS. I stepped closer to join in, as
one does at parties, listened, and contributed a thought.
These were friends. One was a close friend. They looked
at me, didn't say a thing, then looked back at each other,
shared a knowing smile and continued on…as if I'd
never been there.

My thoughts are too oddball even for my own friends.

I have a beautiful family. We have a nice suburban
house, in a nice suburban neighborhood. We have beautiful kids, dogs, cats, neighbors. Over the years I took
part-time jobs. I delivered the New York Times. I drove
city buses. Then airport busses. Then tour busses. I
worked in the newsroom at a local newspaper. I even
went back to school, briefly. The jobs were mostly part-
time, but sometimes full-time, as the kid situation allowed. No 'career.' None of the jobs paid much. School
fizzled. I couldn't see myself doing anything that an 'ed-
ucation' would get me. Call it lack of imagination. Then
one day, when the kids were old enough that they didn't
need me at home all the time, I saw a sign for a trucking
school. Handy! A million-plus trucking miles later, I'm
still at it.

So, I look back at the arc of my own life, and tell myself the story of my life, and it all leads to here. Where I
am. Which of course is the only place it could lead, if I
am to be 'me,' but on the other hand, it's the place I have
to be, to be *who I am*.

It's not a 'control' thing. It's a 'who I am' thing. I
'control' who I am, by *being* who I am.

Character is destiny
—Heraclitus (535–475 BC)

One day we got a call from my cousin. My favorite aunt, the second oldest of nine Irish kids, was gone. Ninety-plus years old, she'd been sitting at a bar having drinks with friends, when someone looked and realized she wasn't responsive. She was rushed to a hospital, but that was pretty much that, for her.

The very next day, no kidding, we got a call from my dad's wife. Dad, the second youngest of those same nine Irish kids, had cancer. Only weeks later, and he too was gone, the last of the nine to go.

All those stories, gone.

Dad and I talked on the phone almost every week when he was still with us, but never for long. It was a rare conversation with Dad that lasted more than five minutes. He always had something going on, something to do. That's what he said. And a lot of times I believed him. He had a warehouse in Deerfield Beach, across the street from the warehouses he used to lease back in the 1970s when he was juggling three construction crews between four or five different construction sites, working a string of jobs from South Carolina to the Virgin Islands. Air-conditioned offices are extra in the warehouse-biz, but he had one. He was the owner's on-site agent, which got him that warehouse rent-free. He kept all his tools there and spent all day, every day, designing circuits, building circuits, troubleshooting circuit boards. If you looked in the local yellow pages you'd find him listed there, under 'Inventors.'

There's always a last time. The last time Dad went to work he took his three boys with him. He was having trouble concentrating by then, so we did the work for him, under his direction. It was like being 15 again, except I was 55. "Don't *try* to do it, Johnny, just *do* it!"

"Okay Dad, got it!"

It was great, actually. All of us together again, working together again for a common cause, lacking only Mom, for one last time. Bittersweet, of course, because we all knew he wouldn't be with us long. And he wasn't. And when the undertakers came over, to pick up the body, the one man, a big guy, found himself with tears running down his face, right there in the apartment.

What are the chances? He used to service the vending machines around that warehouse district, and would stop in to settle accounts with my dad, and said he always enjoyed the banter, and the stories my dad used to tell.

There was a 'hippie' wave that washed over the universe of the Western world in the 1960s and '70s, The dawn of the 'Age of Aquarius.' Bell bottoms. Flower children. It didn't last long. I didn't get caught up in it. But regardless of how drug-fueled and/or naïve you may judge the movement to have been, it was real, in the sense that it tapped into an egalitarian undercurrent that feeds Life. Human Life. *All* Life.

Wave and particle, awareness and creation: these are metaphors. Life is a metaphor. Every element of Life is reflected metaphorically, somehow, in every other element of Life. It's a 'world in a grain of sand' kind of thing, and from that perspective we're all the same. We're all 'equal.'

Particles, when we look closely at them, can seem so different, so wildly different even, from other particles. Some particles we might judge to be 'beautiful,' and others 'not so beautiful,' while others might seem downright ugly. We make judgments about the particles we experience, and ultimately, in judging the particles we know, we judge the particle we know as our 'self,' as well, and we do so from inside the boundary of an equation of 'beauty' that we ourselves have created or adopted as our own.

We have to. We don't have a choice. To be a 'particle'—to exist as a thing—is to exist as a thing different from other things, or it's not to exist at all. Yet all those 'particles,' each of us our own, from a wider perspective they are all part of a wave, equal. A wave exists as a relationship between particles, not as the particles themselves. To that degree, there are no 'particles'; there are only relationships.

When you see a wave flowing across a stadium, do you see people? Or a wave?

It's a perspective thing, sure; the people are there, but 'individuality' is gone to the point that there are no individuals; there is only that flowing wave. There's almost a magical quality to it.

We are all equal, and we are all individual, all at once, at the same 'time.'

Democracy, at its core, is based on egalitarian principles: one person, one vote, all equal. But in this winner/loser, competition capitalist world of ours, ideas like 'worth,' and 'status,' are seductive, and in succumbing to them, we lose sight of that essential truth that we are all equal. *And* individual.

'Worth,' 'status,' 'winner,' 'loser': these are 'moral strata' words based at root not solely on the idea of levels, and layers, like a cake, or tree rings, but on a judgment of those levels and layers. Some levels are 'better' than others. And we all see that: upper-class, middle-class, lower-class, for example. And maybe we can congratulate ourselves if we don't buy into any notion that there is something 'better' about being rich. Money is not a gauge of moral worth. But where would you rather your child end up, as the janitor at the courthouse, or as the judge whose courtroom needs cleaning?

Life is a metaphor of itself. It reflects itself over and over again. We make so much of our leaders, of the Big People of our world, the movers, the shakers. And to the extent that these movers and shakers possess qualities that we may want to emulate, that's a fine thing. But we forget, in making so much of them, the simple example of a pyramid. That capstone, the one at the very top? It only exists as the pinnacle of the pyramid because the rest of the pyramid also exists. Meaning, that capstone is beholden to the rest of the pyramid for its very existence.

In a pyramid, every stone works to support the stones above it, and is itself supported by the stones below. In the pyramid of a courthouse, as an example, the janitor helps the judge to be a judge. Without a workable courtroom, the judge can't be a judge. So in that sense, like a stone in a pyramid supporting the stones above it, the janitor serves as an integral part of the judge's work.

Some positions in a society—it is very true— are more difficult. Like that janitor. It's not easy being at the low end of everyone's totem pole. Ask any janitor, if, given the gift of learning—and the love of status that most judges have—would they rather have been a judge, if only to please their mother? Most would probably say 'yes.' Ask a judge the same thing, would they rather, *every working day*, hold in their hands a mop, or a gavel?

If it is so difficult being a janitor, that no one wants to be one, why do we so often dismiss those who do that entirely necessary job, as less than worthy?

Is your lower intestinal tract less worthy than your upper respiratory tract, because one deals with air, and the other something else?

"Blessed are the meek, for they will inherit the earth"
—Jesus of Nazareth

The meek possess a sure and hidden strength of which their overseers have no need: hope.

It seems to be built into our very genes, because it happens again and again: those who have, have few children; those who have not, have many children. By this equation alone, the meek shall always inherit the Earth, if only by force of numbers.

But revolution—a force of numbers rising up against a force of arms—that's an ugly, bloody, transformation.

When we look at the world, and see it built not from the top-down, alone, but from all sides at once, each living element exerting itself, being Life, that's when we can fully appreciate the contribution of all humans, be they slave or master, janitor or judge, teamster or emperor, that's when we can see that each individual contributes *equally*, not by dint of hours logged at labor, but by dint of hours logged as human.

Human society.

Perhaps, as a species, we can learn to view our organizations not as a celebration of whatever human capstone might dance at the top of the pile, but as a testament instead to the contribution of each and every block of whatever construction we might be inspired to build, built true, built bold, built by all, a testament to each of us.

It's only when we understand that the true glory and nature of a pyramid is that it is a construction supported equally by all, that all will benefit from the pyramid.

All who live true to others, and thus to themselves and to Life, are worthy, equally.

Groovy!

7

CHANGE

February 2017

A navy buddy let me borrow his muscle-car Camaro…once. Maybe not a smart move. He'd done a lot of custom work on that engine, and car, and I pulled the muffler off when the car bottomed out on a *tiny* little dip on a freeway on-ramp. I'd never noticed that tiny dip before. I'd never been doing 80 mph on that on-ramp before either. The car went one way; the muffler went another…

That car was loud *with* a muffler.

My buddy laughed and laughed when I told him the story. I was ridiculously embarrassed, but he wouldn't take any money for it. Wouldn't hear of it. And apologized to *me* for not warning me that the muffler was hung maybe a little low. What a guy!

But that acceleration…

What is that, anyway, 'acceleration'? In unit terms it equals 'velocity divided by time,' so, it's a measure of how much faster (or slower—'negative' acceleration) a thing is going from one moment to the next. Small point, but, any change in direction is also an acceleration, like steering around a corner (it feels the same, doesn't it?). And we all know acceleration. We've all *felt* acceleration. But what is *that*? What is it to 'feel' something?

Remember the unit-particle, a particle complete unto itself, existing in a universe of that particle and nothing else besides? If we added another unit-particle to that singular universe, we could then compare the two, and determine, perhaps, qualities of both that existed in terms of the relationship between the two.

For starters, we could put the second particle immediately next to the first one, for a direct, no-nonsense size comparison. Then we could stop all motion, freeze time, in effect, so there is no relative motion between them, nothing to complicate the issue. And if one particle is significantly shorter or longer or whatnot, from the other, we'd have established one aspect, at least—that of relative size in one or more dimensions—of the relationship between the two unit-particles.

And that works—until we bring in someone else, and show them our universe of two unit-particles.

We've defined this system of ours as a 'system of two unit-particles,' so, for us, that's what it is. But, if we bring in a third party, and have them observe our unit-particle universe, unless we tell them that this is a universe of 'two unit-particles,' is there any way for this third party to know, for sure, that these 'two unit-particles' *are* two unit-particles, or even just two things? They're right next to each other, unmoving, unchanging. Is there any way to tell them apart?

Silly question?

I have an uncle, my mom's older brother, Lester William Scharf, my Uncle Bill, who has made a living selling his art and teaching art in New York City for going on seven decades. Personally, I love his stuff. It speaks to me of a kind of alternative, emotional world of color, texture, and symbol, but no place to put your finger and say, 'ah ha!' Like music of no words, painted unchanging on a canvas.

The titles can be intriguing: 'The Golden Anchor Escapes'; 'The Dawn Between the Weapons'; 'Ascending Betrayal.'

There is undeniable deliberation to his art. Indeed, I've seen him map out his creations ahead of time, drawing, drawing, very carefully, even sitting at breakfast there is a pad at his side. So I've taken to wondering, what if we could animate his paintings? Give them motion?

The thing about my uncle's paintings is that there are recurring shapes, and forms, but connections? Is it all one thing? Are there any 'things'? You can ask him questions about his work, about what is 'this' supposed to be, or even if it's supposed to be, or represent, anything, and, well, the question will kind of echo in the room, and that will have to serve as your answer.

If the thoughts of my uncle were magically instilled in his paint, as he brushed it on his canvas, and if we could animate this paint, could we then see, not the thoughts direct, but the connections, the relationships between the colors, the forms, the tensions of the work? This 'dab of red,' over there, now moves over here, so perhaps it's a coherent thing, a thing unto itself. Given enough time, and change, we might be able to map a pattern of relationships for the entire work.

Would that work?

Or, as a different example, we might see a painting of a distant sailing ship at sea in a storm, and we know, we have contextual experience, that we're looking at something that's supposed to be a ship with sails and yardarms and crew, and another thing that's supposed to be the ocean and waves and wind, so we bring to that painting our own expectations, our own feelings about storms, and lonely ships at sea. But without that contextual experience, what would we be looking at?

The point is, without 'change,' without a changing relationship between the elements of Life, lacking contextual experience there is no way to tell what the nature of any relationship is, or indeed if there is any 'relationship' at all, even of something as simple as relative size. Even for oneself.

Imagine, for example, that every time you opened your eyes there was a couch to your left—in your peripheral vision perhaps, and just out of reach, but it was always there. Everywhere you went, and no matter how you turned your head, looking exactly the same and in exactly the same place in relation to your head, there was that couch. Would you start to feel, after a while, that the couch and you were the same thing?

> *"You've got flies in your eyes...that's probably why you can't see them"*
> **—Yossarian, in *Catch-22*, by Joseph Heller (Simon & Schuster, 1961)**

Two things, existing in a relationship unchanging, become one thing. It is 'change' itself, in a way, that differentiates 'things,' allowing things to exist as 'things' apart.

The wider point I'm trying to make, badly, is that without change, there is no Life. No existence. No 'things'! Which might strike you as stupid: Yeah, duh! Heart stops! But...

> *I also take it as granted that every created thing...is subject to change, and indeed that this change is continual in each one*
> **—Gottfried Wilhelm Leibniz (1646–1716)**

> *Nothing endures but change*
> **—Heraclitus (535–475 BC)**

What *is* 'change'?

We're all familiar with 'speed.' Once you're 'at speed,' is there any way to know you are? Once you're at cruising altitude in a jet airplane, on a smooth flight, even going 500 mph, if you can't look out the window, if you can't gauge your position in relation to something else, can you tell you're moving? Can you *feel* yourself moving? (Even if you can gauge your motion in relation to something else, can you know, for sure, that it's *you* moving, and not the other thing?)

My submarine was like that too. We'd cruise for days—or weeks—underwater, with no way of knowing (without access to the navigation information) how fast we were moving, what direction we were moving in, or even if we were moving at all. Sometimes we'd go to periscope depth, and the whole boat would take on a mild 'up angle,' like climbing a hill, and when we got just below the surface of the ocean we'd level off, and sometimes the boat would roll a little (or a lot!), depending on how rough the conditions were topside. Then we'd go back down, and the boat would take on a little down angle, like going downhill, and then...nothing. Solid as a house. Sometimes we'd crank in some power, put on some extra speed, and the boat would vibrate, especially aft in the engineering spaces. And at flank (top) speed, the whole boat would shake, stem to stern, which was wild, but other than that, at normal cruising speeds, no motion. Nothing. There could be a typhoon raging topside and if we were deep enough, we wouldn't feel a thing. It was a little weird.

The first time on a transit, I went down the engine room hatch in bright daylight in San Diego; lived and worked for a week in a strange and welded-together machinery world, feeling virtually no external motion; and, climbing up through the same engine room hatch, found myself in bright daylight in Pearl Harbor. After climbing down through the hatch in San Diego, it was like emerging into an alternate universe. That was what was weird, no 'change,' no real perception of motion, and then, Hawaii!

Nice alternate universe...

It says it right in Newton's first law of motion: 'An object at rest stays at rest, and an object in motion stays in motion, with the same speed and in the same direction *unless acted upon by an external force*' (emphasis mine). Put another way, motion, all by itself, isn't 'change.'

Energy, funny to think of it this way, but it doesn't actually *do* anything. Like money in the bank, it…sits there. It's an asteroid speeding through deep space, all that speed, all that stored energy of motion, but not doing anything with it, just…moving. It's when that money gets spent, when that asteroid hits something, that's when the 'work' gets done. That's when things get accelerated, and that's what you have to do to 'change' something, change its speed and/or direction—otherwise known as changing its 'momentum' (we're talking about kinetic energy here, the energy of motion). And that's where 'force' comes in.

Per Newton's second law of motion, force equals 'mass times acceleration': $F=ma$. Modern physics prefers, 'the instantaneous rate of change of momentum with respect to time.' Either way, when you accelerate a mass, like, say, throwing a baseball, you've changed its momentum—you've exerted 'force.'

Interestingly, you've also changed yourself, because 'for every action, there is an equal and opposite reaction': that's Newton's third law of motion.

When you accelerate a thing, like throwing a ball, you have to brace yourself to throw it because you're also accelerating yourself, in the opposite direction. In terms of momentum ('mass times velocity'), the force you exert on the ball works to throw you backward by the identical amount that it works to throw the ball forward, with the net effect that all that 'force' cancels out. Which only makes sense, because if nothing else is accelerating, then there is nothing else being 'forced.' And it's for that very reason that physicists often use the term 'interaction' instead of 'force.' Which also makes sense.

'Force,' the word, while it may be defined in terms of 'units'—an equation—still, in our heads it conjures up metaphorical images. 'Force' images. And force, in our head, is a kind of one-way street, a bat hitting a ball kind of thing, or your dad, maybe, banging on a misaligned metal fence post bracket with a sledgehammer, while you stand inches away. "I'm not going to hit you with the hammer, Johnny! Push on that bolt and slide it in when I bang on this bracket and 'force' this thing into place! Just do it!" Thanks, Dad, for not hitting me with that hammer.

But 'interaction'? It seems so...passive. Force is something that happens! Mountains being 'forced' into existence by shifting tectonic plates. Muscle cars being 'forced' forward by great gobs of unneeded horsepower! That kind of stuff. Big stuff. Man stuff!

'Interaction'? That's kind of girlish, isn't it? But really, that's what 'force' is all about—a relationship.

So, you're walking in the door at work, and here's your boss (sycophant entourage in attendance around her), heading out the door. She spies you, slows, and with one quick sentence changes all your weekend plans: "I'm pushing up the meeting to first thing Monday."

It's an interaction, a change in relationship.

Behind you as you slowed were three other people, but they didn't stop, and you were too stunned, perhaps, to even notice them; they walked right on past. No 'interaction.'

Or, imagine two different armies on the same road, marching toward each other. Oh no! Will they battle? Nope. Peacetime maneuvers; no body bags. They squeeze up and slide past each other. Minor interactions only.

Or, a construction foreman coming back from a meeting, and here's his crew heading out to lunch, ten minutes early. He takes one look, makes one arm motion, and the whole crew spins on its heels, back to work. Solid interaction.

Okay, now, substitute atoms and molecules for people: And it's you, a beta particle, changing direction after interacting with an atom (swirling electrons in attendance around it).

It's three neutrinos, speeding past, not interacting with anything.

It's an army of vinegar, sliding past another army of oil, poured into a bowl.

It's the crystalline steel of a hammer, the foreman, pounding that fence post crew back into place.

If that hammer didn't 'interact' with that fence post, if there wasn't a solid 'relationship' between the two, it would slide right through it. It would be like hitting smoke, except that even smoke gets out of the way. If there is no interaction, at all, if there is no relationship, then getting out of the way isn't a part of it. If there is no 'interaction,' there is no change, there is no acceleration.

So, to answer the question, what is 'change'? It's an *interaction*. And an interaction, any interaction, no matter how big, or small, is reflected in atomic level events.

Atoms, accelerating.

8

FEELING

February 2017

There is nothing incorporeal, insubstantial, other-worldly, *immaterial* in our kinetic whirl. If it exists, there is a reason for it to exist, as it exists, where it exists, in the condition in which it exists. And if a thing doesn't exist...

What is there to say, of the nonexistent?

(Is it possible to 'interact' with the nonexistent?)

Even a 'relationship' exists. It's not immaterial. Just because it seems that you can't touch it, or see it, or smell it, doesn't mean it's not there. Because you are touching it. You are feeling it. A relationship is felt in your skull, in your gut, in the cells of which you are composed—30 trillion of them, give or take an order of magnitude, so maybe 3, or maybe 300...*trillion*...cells. Trillion, with a 't.' (If you were a cell, and you lived for 30 thousand microseconds, you'd live for 30 seconds; if you lived for 30 trillion microseconds, you'd live for 950 years.)

'Feeling' is real. A 'relationship' is a real thing. What is 'real' about a 'relationship,' that we can feel it?

Any relationship, just like our universe of two unit-particles, requires change—interaction—to exist as a 're-lationship.' But in this kinetic whirl of a universe in which we exist, we take 'change' for granted. We don't

79

see it, even when we're looking straight at it, like at our own stationary image in the mirror. Even standing stock still, interactions are occurring. The very photons we use to 'see' ourselves are interacting, via electromagnetic waves interacting with atoms in the mirror, and with us, with our eyes. That pimple or wrinkle we're staring at may not be going away anytime soon, but time is passing. Electrons are swirling. Hearts are beating.

The point is, change doesn't have to be big, to be real.

When those words were spoken, 'Dad passed away last night in his sleep,' what happened, to me? What 'changed,' for me, to 'feel'—anything?

The simple stupid answer: pressure waves of air interacted with my ears, and I 'heard,' I experienced, those pressure waves as words, coded into the very way the air vibrated.

And after I negotiated the manicured walkways of the Pompano Beach condominium complex, bright, green grass, palm trees, and hibiscus, and entered the building's marvelously slow, sticky-humid elevator, and went up to the apartment, and saw my dad there, or what used to be 'my dad,' on the hospice-provided hospital bed—an immaculately clean, Florida bedroom with a dead body in it—what happened to me?

Electromagnetic waves, light waves, interacting with the form on the bed, 'reflected' off it toward me, and then interacted with my eyes. Again, very mechanistic seeming. And indeed, we could take that 'mechanism' further by thinking of it in terms of an information storage and retrieval system. The form on the bed 'stored' information; and that information was 'retrieved,' by me, via photons, interacting with my eyes.

And it all might seem a sad and unfeeling way of looking at it. But really, it's not. Not at all. Because that's what we're getting at.

What *is* 'feeling'? What is it to *feel*?

It's so easy to get caught up in 'response.' The world can seem so straightforward when we look at it in terms of 'response': cause generating an effect, input generating output. Like a watch, we wind it up and...response-tick, response-tock...

It can seem so straightforward because, simple reason, that's what we've been taught that Life is, mechanistic, so that's how we 'see' it. But to view the panorama of Life as a kind of grand machine, biological or not, leads to all kinds of questions, like: Do we have free will? What is it to be conscious? What is awareness?

I was once startled from a deep sleep when something, something *big*, brushed across the top of my head. I was alone at the time, asleep in a dark room...

It was a sultry, humid Florida night in May. The windows were open. I don't think we had air conditioning in that once-proud, but now run-down old house my family was renting at the time. We'd recently lost Mom's dream home to the bank, and I'd moved out of my apartment and was living with my family for a few days before going on a road trip to see the U.S.A.—all the way to California and back again—a trip I'd been saving for all year.

Mom, I'll never forget, being a mom, that morning that I left, she came running outside in her nightgown at 4 a.m. I was already backing out of the driveway, car all loaded up, but she had a big package of paper napkins under her arm. We'd said goodbye in the house, but here she was, running barefoot on the concrete. "You might need these Honey!" she said, passing them through the car window to me. I didn't want them, but she insisted, pushing them in at me. "You're going to need them!"

She was very insistent.

Moments like that? What can you say about moments like that? You want them back! So you can grab your mom's hand and hold it, just for a moment, maybe, but, a moment that would last a lifetime.

Life is the experience of it.

She was right about those paper napkins, by the way. I used every one.

But, back to the story. I'd fallen asleep with my arm up above my head. And the whole thing, shoulder on down, fell asleep. Dead, meat, asleep. So, when I moved, I suspect, I felt this big thing touching my head, and it freaked me out, because while my hand couldn't feel anything, including my head, my head could sure feel something!

I sat up in the pitch dark, half in a panic, wondering what was up, and something slid across my thigh!

There was some animal in the room with me! That's what was going through my head. The room was dark as pitch. The closest light switch was on the wall across the room. I called out, "Get away!" jumped up and twisted violently sideways to get away from this thing, whatever it was, and it hit me across the chest. I twisted the other way and it hit me across the back! Hard!

Not joking. True story. I was beating myself up with my own numb arm, in the dark, and didn't know it. No feeling at all. When I finally got the light on, there it was, hanging, floppy and useless. That was freaky all on its own.

But, what if not just that arm, but my other arm too, had no feeling? And my legs, torso, head: no feeling? No feeling of warmth, or cold. No feeling of hunger, or pain. No feeling of comfort, or joy.

No sight. No sound. No thoughts.

No feeling.

Nothing.

Imagine a single-cell organism. It comes upon a morsel of silica, and ignores it. Now it comes upon a morsel of protein, and eats it.

What's the difference? How did 'it' 'know' to ingest the protein, and not the silica?

We pride ourselves as humans on having an 'objective' perspective, a kind of lens that allows us to look at our world as if from a remove, as if separate from it. We call this lens, rather haughtily, 'mind,' 'being,' or 'consciousness.' We assume that it takes this lens for us to be 'aware' of our actions and to 'know' that we 'exist' in a 'world.' And because we're the only beings (we know of) who possess such a lens, then only we humans are 'aware.'

By this thinking our single-cell organism isn't 'aware'; like the watch—response-tick, response-tock—it 'automatically' ingests the protein and ignores the silica. And by this thinking that's what happens in our bodies as well: air vibrates in ear, eardrums 'detect' the vibration, and so on. But at some point, it might seem, looking at all of it, the smells, the sights, the sounds, through my own 'objective lens' I became—somehow—'aware' that Dad was dead.

What is that 'somehow'? How does a 'response' become an 'awareness'? Is it a matter of complication, complexity, connection? That seems to be the current consensus take on it. Modern machines, it seems, may be on the cusp of achieving 'consciousness.' It's all so complex, this world of ours, there are so many 'connections,' that it might seem to make sense that at some point the internet, perhaps, would put it all together and...understand!

After high school, but before college, I took a year off and got my own apartment. I made $4 per hour and for $140 a month, no kidding, rented a clean set of furnished rooms all to myself over a stand-alone backyard garage a block off Fort Lauderdale's hoity-toity Las Olas Boulevard (amazing, dismaying thing, inflation—and uneven wealth accumulation). It was a bit of a commute to my job in Deerfield Beach, and I quickly learned not to trust electric alarm clocks, because, if the power went out (like, when I didn't pay the bill), so did the clock. So, I bought an inexpensive, wind-up alarm clock, and for many years it gave me reliable, no-directions-required,

no-frills use; I just had to make sure to wind it up periodically. Now, I have a cell phone to do that job; I just
have to make sure to charge it periodically. Sure, the cell
phone is slightly more complicated, but at least in terms
of wake-up alarms, it does the same job. Indeed, both
devices follow the same laws of physics.

The amazing thing about that, is that that's not amazing. What is amazing, is that we humans, each of us
'made' of our 30 trillion (with a 't') cells—so, yeah,
we're slightly more complicated than a single-cell organism—but, despite our oh-so-complex brains, we can't
seem to get it through all those myriad connections
we're so proud of that maybe it's likely that just as cell
phones follow the same 'rules' of physics as windup
clocks, we too, living beings that we are, might follow
the same 'rules' of Life, as single-cell organisms.

Life is Life. Right?

If that's the case, that Life is Life, then maybe it might
be possible that just as we can be 'aware' of hunger,
when we are hungry, then maybe a single-cell organism
could also be aware of hunger, when it is hungry.

Make sense?

But of course, single-cell organisms don't have 'brains'
(among other objections) so how could 'it' 'know' 'it'
was 'hungry'?

You wouldn't know it by looking at them, but truckers are very weight conscious—of their rigs. Eighty
thousand pounds is the gross vehicle weight restriction
on federal highways, but individual axles are limited as
well. Place a 48,000-pound load of bricks one foot too
far forward or back on a trailer deck, and you might be
1,200 pounds over on an axle weight. And that ticket,
from a highway scale? It's gonna hurt. Maybe a week's,
maybe two week's take-home pay for the driver, depending.

There is a myth in the world of truckers that weight at
the back of the trailer is 'felt' on the trailer axles (at the

rear), and weight at the front of the trailer is 'felt' on the drive axles (under the front of a trailer, on a semi-trailer).

And it seems to make sense to look at it that way, because it seems there is some balance point on the trailer, like on a teeter-totter, and so weight placed to the right of this imaginary balance point moves the right side down, and weight on the left moves the left side down, and so on. Between the few hundred pounds of leeway the highway patrol will give you (not out of the goodness of their hearts, necessarily, but probably more to do with the calibration range of their scales), and the fact that you're usually a little under max gross weight to begin with, and most of the time that 'myth' works just fine.

Most of the time.

In the flatbed trailer world I'm familiar with 'center-loaded' loads are the most notorious. They're bunched in the center of the trailer, with any extra space on the deck split front and back. Pallets in the middle of such a load are squeezed in; they won't slide out once loaded. And if you pick up a 3,600-pound pallet from the back of a center-loaded load, and move it to the front of that load, you're moving it a long way. In fact, you're probably moving your overweight axle problem off one set of axles, onto another set. But what else can you do, other than unload an entire trailer, and then reload it in a slightly different spot? (And I've seen guys do just that.)

There often is that extra deck space, but moving a 3,600-pound pallet six feet or so from the front of a center-loaded load, to the front of the trailer? Is that going to help an overweight condition 40 feet or more away at the *back* of the trailer? How could it help? It's all the way at the back!

That's how most drivers will look at it. They won't even try it, because the metaphor is stuck in their head: weight on the back, is weight on the back; weight on the front, is weight on the front. So, moving weight in the front, to the front, doesn't help the back!

And yet…

It does.

Move a front pair of 3,600-pound pallets six feet forward, and you've moved better than 1,200 pounds off rear axles almost 40 feet away. How? Simple. It's not two trailers magically split in the middle at a 'balance point.' It's one trailer, that *distributes* weight, front and back.

So, what does this have to do with anything?

Metaphors!

The metaphors we choose about our world work to shape the story we tell ourselves about our world. To change the world we see, we need to change the metaphors we use. Like, for example, the metaphors we use about awareness, because to be aware is a feeling—the feeling of being aware—and 'feelings,' like a trailer that doesn't have a boundary splitting 'front' from 'back,' well, feelings too don't have boundaries. More to the point, feelings, to be 'felt,' don't *need* boundaries.

And that's kind of literally true, isn't it? Your feelings about your mom, for example, aren't bounded somehow, split between 'this' part of your world, and 'that' part of your world. Are they?

Or a prick of the finger. It hurts! You will need a brain, certainly, and a sense of self to compose a sentence about it, "Oh dear! I have pricked my little finger." But, to *feel* the pain? Are any boundaries, of 'self,' or 'I,' required? Did those newborn pups of Hildi's, blind and all but helpless, did they need to 'know' they were 'alive,' to know they were hungry? From the way they relentlessly fought and squirmed to get to their mother's milk, you sure wouldn't think so!

To be aware, then, is to feel. To be aware of hunger, is to *feel* hunger. To be aware of a mirror is to *feel* the mirror (with your eyes). To be aware of salt is to *feel* the salt (with your tongue, or your fingers, or your eyes).

So, that's our new metaphor: awareness is a feeling. And maybe we used some iffy reasoning to arrive at that, but let's run with it anyway, and see where it leads, and in the meantime we can work out this little hanging question: what is it to 'feel'?

If we run with this new metaphor, it allows us to re-examine some things, like our very language. Because language? It's its own short-circuit. Words encapsulate ideas. String a bunch of words together and we're driving a freeway of thought, and like any freeway you can only get off at the designated exits.

'Organism,' is a word. To be a word it must have a definition. Definitions must demarcate—split things off from other things. So, to say an 'organism' is 'aware' of, say, a morsel of protein, seems to grant a separate, demarcated existence to that 'organism,' one that allows 'it' to 'be' 'aware.' But, just like in our universe of two unit-particles, simply defining a thing, as a thing, doesn't make it a thing, except in our own minds.

Thinking of 'awareness' as a 'feeling' allows us to get off our freeway of thought at a new exit, newly formed, one that leads to the thought that maybe it is possible to be aware of a thing, without the need to 'be' a 'thing' that 'knows' that 'it' is 'aware' of a 'thing.'

There is just, the feeling.

Maybe it is possible to feel 'hunger,' for example, without any inkling that there is a 'me' that is 'hungry.' There is just the feeling, one we call 'hunger.'

'Hunger,' then, can be an experience independent of thought, independent of 'I,' and 'self,' or even of any 'agent' at all, any 'being' that needs to 'exist' in order to 'be' 'hungry.' There is just the feeling, *hunger*.

By this reckoning, 'hunger' (or any feeling), is its own medium of existence. More or less like a light wave, existing, in a sense, as its own medium, lacking any external 'aether,' or agent, feeling *is* existence.

If feeling is existence, if it exists as its own thing, that allows us to unlink 'awareness' from any kind of defining boundary. No longer does a 'thing' (like an organism) need to 'exist' as a prerequisite for 'it' to be 'aware.'

It frees us, as well, to think of awareness as a kind of 'indicator of change,' unrelated to thought.

If we do that, then even a single-cell organism can possess 'awareness' of change. Just like we do, it *feels* change.

But language, again, can get in the way, because to say that an organism can 'possess awareness' is perhaps to misapprehend the concept. It's not that a thing 'possesses' awareness, it's that the thing *is* awareness—awareness of being a thing.

Put another way, to be aware of being a thing, is to be a thing. To be aware of being a thing with a cat on your lap, is to be a thing with a cat on your lap.

We're making relationships 'real.' Awareness is its own 'thing,' its own medium. It exists in and of itself. Awareness is also an indicator of change. When you hear something, you are aware of that change via your hearing; when you see something, you are aware of that change via sight; when you *think* of something you are aware of that change via your thoughts. And if you are aware of any of that, of anything, anything at all, even of a couch in the corner of your eye or flies in the eyes of someone else, then something has changed, somewhere, so as to make you aware.

In our kinetic whirl of a universe, change, *any* change, anywhere, of any nature, manifests at some level as an interaction. Something, somewhere, even if it's just an electron, got accelerated. And to accelerate something, anything, an interaction must occur.

Interaction—force—takes energy. That's why you get tired even just sitting at a desk all day using 'brainpower' to make a paycheck, because there is actual 'power' involved in thinking. Power is a measure of how quickly energy is being transferred (from one 'energy bank' account to another, in a metaphorical sense). Where energy has been transferred, force has been exerted. Where force is exerted, things get accelerated, and momentums get changed.

To put it succinctly, to be aware (as I'm aware of it!), is to be aware of change(s) in momentum, specifically (or so I suspect) in an electromagnetic field. Like, in an atom, where photons come from. (Did I just make us each the light of our own life? Your call.)

> *"You're off the edge of the map, mate. Here there be monsters"*
> **—Barbossa, in *Pirates of the Caribbean: The Curse of the Black Pearl* (2003)**

And so we've come to the 'inside-out' part.

Life is a metaphor. It's like an image where if you 'see' the one color, it outlines one thing, but if you 'see' the other color, a different thing gets outlined.

Do you see it?

A vase in black becomes the profile in white of two faces, looking at each other. A relationship.

What is a 'particle'? When we're talking about an 'electron' or a 'photon,' what are we talking about? Because to call them 'particles' is to use a metaphor. It's to think about them in a way familiar to us. But what are they 'really'? Is there a 'really'?

[T]he atoms or elementary particles themselves are not real; they form a world of potentialities or possibilities rather than one of things or facts
—Werner Heisenberg (1901–1976)

We need words, we need metaphors, but physicists talk of everyday matter being 'made,' more or less, of 'fermions.' A word. While 'bosons,' another word, are the 'glue' (metaphor) that holds that 'matter' (metaphor) together in the required relationships. Bosons are also looked at as 'force carriers,' the means by which momentum is transferred from one 'particle' (metaphor) to another. If force of any type, in any manner, is being applied in our world, then bosons (bless their little bosonic hearts) are on the job, changing that 'relationship' between—interacting with—the fermions. Where would we be without them!

Particles only exist—any 'thing' only exists—in relation to something. And that relation exists as an awareness of that relation. No awareness, no 'thing.' No awareness of a cat on your lap, no cat on your lap. No awareness of an electron, no electron. Simple.

A careful analysis of the process of observation in atomic physics has shown that the subatomic particles have no meaning as isolated entities, but can only be understood as interconnections between the preparation of an experiment and the subsequent measurement
—Erwin Schrödinger (1887–1961)

A boson, then, can be thought of as 'carrying' awareness, defining the relationship between fermions.
Boson/fermion: universe.

How would you feel, if you had no feeling?

We tend to think of 'awareness' as coming all at once, in a package, so to speak. We are aware of friends, dogs, dinner, coffee cups, tables, of entire situations, and so on. But 'awareness' comes in pieces, one at a time: angle, corner, surface, leg…when we get enough pieces we can 'put it together' into a single 'awareness': table! Maybe it only takes microseconds to 'assemble' the 'pieces' (for most things), but nonetheless that putting-together part, no matter how long it takes, that's our story, our interpretation. We call it a 'table,' but 'table,' ultimately, is an interpretation, not a thing coherent of itself. Is an upside-down 'dining table' still a table? Can you dine at it? Would you even recognize it? Or, the empty cable reel I took from work, in my job after I left college: why wasn't it a 'table' when I found it in the dumpster, but when I put it in my new apartment, in front of the gold couch (on the—no kidding—bright red, wall-to-wall, shag, carpet), magically it became, "Nice coffee table!"

How does 'not a table,' become 'table'?

Interpretation. Story.

The point is, 'awareness' is not a given; it's a relationship by relationship construction (relationship to us, individually). Just like 'atoms' build 'molecules,' build 'crystals,' build 'metals,' build 'steel,' build 'skyscrapers,' it goes together. We construct an 'awareness' of our world relationship by relationship. Relationship by relationship this world is built. And still we're not seeing it, are we? We're not seeing it from the 'inside-out' yet, are we?

Maybe we're not singing loudly enough.

Relationship by relationship, awareness by awareness, 'fermion brick' by 'fermion brick,' 'boson glue' by 'boson glue,' this world is built. It's the 'stuff' of which it's made, atoms, molecules, everything.

'Fermion' by 'fermion,' 'relationship between fermions' by 'relationship between fermions,' this world is built. 'Awareness' by 'awareness' of those relationships, this world is built.

'Feeling' by *'feeling'* of those changing relationships, this world is built.

Bosons: they're like little pinpoints of feeling—that's more or less how I've taken to thinking of them (or at least, feeling 'potentials'). That's my metaphor for them.

They're like teeny-weeny 'change transmitters,' telling us, if we can 'hear' it, that *'this changed'* and *'that changed,'* and *'this other thing changed'*—Life *feels* them, tiny little lighthouse flashes of awareness potential held in place, held in relationship to each other, by those fermions, forming patterns of feeling with every acceleration, every interaction, trillions upon trillions upon trillions of them...

Life!

What would you feel, if you had no feeling? Even thoughts are 'felt'; they're feelings, felt in the brain. But if you had none...

If you didn't feel, anything, what would you be?

The *feeling* that is the change in relationship between all the 'parts' of our world...that is what we are.

If you don't feel a cat on your lap—alive, awake, and aware, if you don't feel a cat on your lap, then there is no cat on your lap.

Alive, awake, and aware, if there is no cat on your lap, then you won't feel a cat on your lap.

The 'feeling' of a cat on your lap, and a 'cat on your lap,' are the same 'thing.'

Life is feeling. Systems of feeling. Patterns of feeling!

Feelings are real. They exist as patterns of relationships, patterns of bosons, patterns of force, patterns of acceleration, of changing momentums, patterns felt in the neurons, connections and so on, in your head, in your gut, in your world.

What are words? Patterns of letters, patterns of sound.

What are digital computers based upon? Patterns of ones, and zeroes.

Just like our conventional wisdom says things are built of other things, atoms building molecules, so too relationships are built of other relationships, patterns of relationships, 'this' series of relationships building 'that' overall relationship. The overall relationship of a thing, to you, is that thing, to you. The relationship and the thing, are the same 'thing.'

Words: they become burdensome.

The way you see—the way you feel about—your spouse, is your spouse, to you. The way you see yourself—the way you feel about yourself—is yourself, to you.

Life is the feeling of it.

That table you sit at is a feeling. The chair you sit in is a feeling. Your history, your memory, is a feeling. Your mom, who she is to you, is a feeling.

Patterns of feelings!

If you don't feel them, how do you interact with them?

They are all 'built' of feelings. Lots of feelings. All yours.

You choose how you feel. You always choose. It's your world. Your interpretation. Your Life. Your feelings. Trillions of them! And more!

Let's not take them for granted.

9

Field of Feeling

April 2017

Do you feel it? Are you aware? Are you seeing it from the inside, looking out?

Me neither.

As an abstraction, yes, I see it. As a gut level understanding, not too much. Too long, probably like you, have I learned and seen Life as objects, as points of 'material,' a world of 'stuff' glued, bolted, welded, chained, fused, screwed, riveted, locked, tied, linked, bedded, together.

Relationship? What is that?

Sixty-year-old truck driver.

I get like this when my brain starts hurting, when the words, writing the words, thinking in words, is too hard, and they don't want to come. I try to find a way in…a new metaphor, a new path, a better path, anything, a language, a word, *anything* that would unlock the door, point the way, provide a threshold over which I could easily step, and see, know, *understand*…

I like driving trucks. I actually do. I've always loved to drive.

I got to know the Los Angeles freeway system during the years I drove over the road, sleeping in the rig, at truck stops, construction sites, parked on the street, or (my favorite) in wide spots on the side of lonely country roads, when after 600 miles you turn off that big, lurching diesel and there's nothing but you, and the cab, and *silence*, the sweetest sound you've ever heard.

But, LA at night, for a driver, wow, when the traffic dissipates it's magic. Exits swirling, entrances feeding, lines guiding, signs pointing, all lit in white, green, red, amber, black of night and stars overhead. Radio off, windows open, rushing desert wind, floating clutches, shifting gears, bouncing, whooshing, diesel *pulling*.

Space is a feeling...

When I think of it as a 'field of feeling,' that's when I come closest, I think, to 'seeing' it. Waves of feeling forming me, being me, the totality of me, me outside of me, the house of me. Everything I know: a feeling. And feeling is something I feel here, not there. Here. Me. Local. So, it all seems self-centered. But you're here too. When I think of you, the reader, and maybe even we've met, but it doesn't matter because you're here with me too. You are a feeling I have. I am a feeling you have. All my world, including you, is me.

Looking at Life as a field of feeling is to see a wave, a continuous pattern of changing relationships. The 'things,' as we know them, such as a table that is hard, a dog that is barking, exist, I think, as a kind of 'overlay.' I feel the sound and overlay it with a label: 'barking dog.' That label, that overlay, exists as a feeling all of its own, draped atop that raw field of feeling.

But that raw field of feeling, unburdened with overlay, with no names or demarcations, that field makes no differentiation 'inside me' or 'outside me.' It's all simply 'feeling.'

The feeling of being hungry doesn't 'exist' only on the inside. When I am hungry, 'hunger' encompasses all my existence. The feeling of a fly, buzzing, doesn't stop at my skin, either. Feeling IS. And when I look at it that way, the cells of which I am 'composed,' they seem to merge, undifferentiated, into the society of which I am a part.

After I started this...odyssey...big word, after I started it, I started doing it backward, and I knew I was. I knew what I was doing, and I knew I was doing it 'wrong.' I was starting at an endpoint. That's what 'absolute responsibility' is. It's the endpoint. From there, starting at the end, starting at where I wanted to end up, where I *had* to end up, for me to be me, I traced a path back through a landscape of thought that had to exist, it seemed to me, if absolute responsibility for oneself was going to be the endpoint.

But I knew something else as well. I don't know how I knew it; I just knew it. I knew it all along. I grew up with it, something I got from both my parents, which is, simply, that we, all of us and each of us, are *valid*.

I don't know how else to put that.

We're real. We each have a perspective that is what we are. Our perspective on Life, the way we look at Life...in communicating it to others we may get it 'wrong,' in understanding it abstractly we may get it 'wrong,' in trying to shape our view to comport with that of others we may get it 'wrong,' but being who we are, a human with a view, a being of Life, we are absolutely right. We are valid.

No one, and nothing, can take that validity away.

If Life for you is God, then God is your Life. If Life for you is a farce, then farcical is your Life. If Life for you is like a box of chocolates, then sweet is your Life. If Life for you is longing for a better Life, then to be ever dissatisfied is your Life.

It's the ultimate metaphor: it is what it is. Each of us live in the world as we see it. The relationship we have with our world *is* our world. The world we feel *is* our world, because no matter how we 'see' it, if that's what we see then that's what we 'feel,' and that's the world that IS. For us. Individually.

We all rock our own boat trying to turn our world into that which we wish it to be, 'feeling' our way.

We can't help it. That's what Life is: the experience of it.

That's how I see it. That's the world that is—for me.

As a little aside, Zeno's famous paradox, the race between Achilles and the tortoise, is easily refuted from an experiential perspective. It also illustrates how metaphors steer our thought processes.

In this footrace, Achilles allows his opponent, the tortoise, a good head start. So, the tortoise starts at point x, and Achilles starts at some point behind point x. The race begins. By the time Achilles reaches point x (where the tortoise started), the tortoise will have reached some point x1, further ahead. And by the time Achilles reaches point x1, the tortoise will have reached some point x2, further ahead from x1. And this will continue, by the logic of this problem, forever. Every time Achilles reaches the point where the tortoise was, the tortoise will have moved ahead of him, so Achilles can never pass the tortoise. Right?

No. Wrong. We know it's wrong, and that's the paradox, but, how?

In this problem, Zeno exploits our current metaphors of space and time. Without saying so, he effectively stops time—in our heads he does—at the point where Achilles would pass the tortoise, but can't, because our current metaphor for length doesn't include that time element. We look at length as an independent dimension of space, and we look at time as progressing independently of experience. But, there can be no meaningful *experience* of length without an experience of time.

As an example, if I were to walk from my front door to the local coffee shop and it took, literally, no time, *at all*, to walk that 'distance,' how 'far' did I walk? Maybe the coffee shop is half a mile away, but, if it takes no time to walk that half a mile, what does 'half a mile' *mean*? Can we have any real experience of 'distance' between two places if we can, effectively, experience both 'places' at once?

Life is the experience of it. If we have no awareness—no experience—of a cat on our lap, is there a cat on our lap? If we have no experience of distance, is there distance? And if we can have no experience of time stopping, can time, for us, stop? Achilles, if he is to experience the 'length' he runs, *must* experience time, and therefore speed in relation to the tortoise.

Space, if we are to *experience* the 'length' of space, requires us to experience 'time' as well, and in all spatial dimensions.

The universe does not 'exist out there' independent of all acts of observation. Instead, it is in some strange sense a participatory universe
—John Archibald Wheeler (1911–2008)

It's a funny thing about that vase, the one 'made' from the 'faces' of a different color on either side, that upon seeing the vase, the faces tend to go away, and upon noticing the faces, the vase tends to go away. It's a perspective thing.

When we venture out the front door of our house of Life, it's helpful to look both ways. It's helpful to see the view from both perspectives because each perspective contributes to the very existence, the very essence of the other.

To see, for example, *only* a world of individuals, of people living in a world that they define as apart from themselves, striving to build a better world for themselves, each alone…it's a fine view. It's the traditional American view, certainly. And for those many of us caught in that perspective, seeing a vase, but no faces, for those of us who value that entrepreneurial, 'against all odds,' 'damn the torpedoes, full speed ahead,' spirit of humanity? That is the world we strive for, to the point that we see *only* the vase, and nothing else besides. Indeed, society can become a 'check your firearms at the door,' 'follow the rules,' 'don't rock the boat,' authoritarian evil, holding us back from our true destiny! Man against nature. Beating the odds. Taking on the world. There is a heroic aspect to it. The 'Spirit of St. Louis' spirit, of the unstoppable, the unalienable, individual!

Sorry for the hyperbole, but, we do romanticize it. And society? Society, as I see it, is not about banks, and bosses, government, and rules; it's about *context*. It's about the context that is the entirety of the world within which each of us find ourselves, because even a wilderness can be 'society.'

If 'wilderness' is the context in which we live, if we are to thrive within a wilderness that is itself thriving, that's the context that we must respect. And that, 'is itself thriving,' is an essential element, because it is all too easy to find, by hard work and determination, sure, but find a way to unlock a well-stocked cupboard, one from which we can then take, and take, and take, without giving back, and calling ourselves all the while 'successful' (for having found and unlocked a well-stocked cupboard). But if that cupboard is not restocked it will in the fullness of time go empty. And that's what 'looking both ways' is all about: respect. Respecting not just our needs within the world, looking to the right, but also the needs of the world of which we are a part, looking to the left. Looking both ways.

Civil liberties, if all cannot equally enjoy them, are not 'civil.'

We get caught up in the wrong, and the right, of our world, as we should!

When I see myself as a particle distinct from 'world,' when I see the vase and not the faces, when the world is 'outside' of me, then morality itself becomes an outside thing. It becomes removed. It becomes a set of rules, laws, commandments, formulated, dictated, promulgated (the military loves that word)—but not necessarily by me.

But what if the cries of others *aren't* the cries of 'others'?

What if the cries of others are part of us, part of our field of feeling, part of our world, our context? Because in a 'field of feeling' there is no 'out there,' there is only 'in here.'

The Catholic Church, famously, asks for confession, which strikes me as an honorable/practical practice. If we push our own actions away, if we make them not part of us, then we can't know who we truly are. And how can we move on to where we'd like to be if we don't admit, at least to ourselves, who and where we are right now?

The flip side of that coin, of confession, is forgiveness. And that only makes sense too, because if in confessing our 'sins'—whether to ourselves or to others—we grasp who we've been, what we've been, what we've done...

It's easy to get caught up in a loop of remorse, which, navigationally speaking, more or less entails getting ourselves even more lost than we previously were.

So, when the cries of others, so piercing, when they come—and they will—and we realize with dismay that those cries are part of who we are, that in a very real way those cries exist *because* of who we are...

Find a way to forgive—yourself.

To exist, at all, is to exist in a context; it's to exist as integral to a time, to a world, to a totality. We can't fix a problem, salve a wound, troubleshoot an issue, without immersing ourselves in those wrongs—immersing ourselves even to the point of becoming the problem, because problems need to be understood to be truly fixed, and there are times when to understand a problem, one must live that problem, and see it from the inside, looking out.

Many cynics will tell you that their gift, and curse, is their ability to see the world as it truly is, thus explaining—if only to themselves—their disdain for it.

The true cynics of the world harbor such unflinching pride in seeing the world 'as it is,' that their greatest fear is being played the fool. With the result that if they, with their unflinching eyes, judge the world to be mercenary, mercenary too they become because 'that's the way the world is,' and they're no one's fool; or, if it is corruption they see, their own corruption they can justify because that's how the game is played, by their rights, and only a fool would play it any other way.

The tragic result is that the world the true cynic builds, is the selfsame world the true cynic disdains: the fool.

Life isn't about problems. Problems are easy to find; they're everywhere.

Life is about *solutions*.

Do unto others as you would have others do unto you
—The Golden Rule

The Golden Rule is not about an absolute set of commandments. It doesn't define, dictate, or constrain. There is no 'do this; don't do that; can't you read the sign...?' aspect to the Golden Rule (from the song by Five Man Electric Band).

Instead, it asks us a question: what kind of a person would we be if we lived in our own more perfect world? It asks us to visualize that more perfect world of ours, and strive to do unto others as if that world *already existed*, because if others would do unto us as we would have them, wouldn't that, then, be our world more perfect?

As you do unto others, so you do unto yourself
—The Golden Rule 2.0

When we come to understand that the world we know is the world *we are*, then this 'Golden Rule 2.0' (which I just made up) makes perfect sense. But, it's hardly a new 'rule':

...you reap whatever you sow
—Galatians 6:7

Translated into a more modern vernacular that biblical quote becomes, '...you harvest what you plant.' In everyday consumerism it reads, 'you get what you pay for.' In urban street: 'what goes around comes around.' And in schoolyard basic: 'turnabout is fair play.'

So, *not a new idea*: we build the world around us. Simple. All we're doing with this book is taking that old idea and moving it along one step further...

We live the world we are.

10

CONSCIOUSNESS

July 2017

Imagine a wide-eyed child, perched high on her daddy's shoulders, watching a parade. She doesn't know what a 'float' is, so she doesn't see 'floats'; she doesn't know what 'bands' are either. To her, that parade, it's an ever-evolving continuum of sounds, of colors, of motion, of fun!

That's the 'field of feeling.'

Or, like a musical album, but one produced with no discernable gap between the songs, the end of one molding itself into the beginning of the next, so no telling where one ends or begins so no real 'songs,' but instead a continuum of *sound*. It's a field of feeling.

It's a leap of understanding, from the experience of a world of 'things' linked together, to a field of feelings inseparable. It's a big leap. But it's what our dog, Charlie, I think that's what she feels, a parade of feelings, largely undifferentiated.

She came to us as a pup. She was found wandering the streets, all happy! Tail wagging! But no collar. No identification. No signs posted. No word left at the pound. Our dog at the time, herself a rescue from the pound, she was getting old. My wife had pronounced, and again and again, "No more dogs!" But when our daughter's best friend brought over that happy, homeless pup, all tail and gangly legs, my wife took one look, and we had a new member of the family.

'Fetch' is Charlie's game. Throw a tennis ball over the roof of the house into the backyard and she's off, full tilt, a headlong rush to find it, fetch it, and in seconds, bring it back! If she can catch it in the air, or on the bounce, all the better. She'll do backflips in the air to catch balls or frisbees.

And when we're done playing, and she knows that because I'll say, "Enough!," that's her cue to dive into her water bowl, get her whole snout into it, and lap up that clear, cold water. And finished she'll look up at me, dripping water, bright of eye, looking right at me.

For me, that's the best part, that eye-to-eye with my dog, and my dog eye-to-eye with her human, *seeing* each other, and she is so, *so* happy.

Sometimes I think those moments, those eye-to-eye moments, are one of the few times that she really does see *me*. In those moments, it seems to me that I become for her a song, a melody with beginning and end, separate unto itself, anchored within the otherwise unending album that is her doggy universe.

I don't know—I don't know that anyone knows, or even can know—how much dogs, or any non-human beings existing in this kinetic whirl that is our universe, 'know' of past or future. To recall a thing, is not necessarily to place that thing as a 'recollection' of the 'past.' But, just as a little mind exercise, imagine it, imagine we exist as a being of no past, or future...

Say, perhaps, we're a gazelle on the wide African savannah, a graceful gazelle, running for dear life, dirt flying off hooves, dodging and weaving, because, well, just because.

We need to run! It's like eating, we need to eat when we need to eat. We need to drink when we need to drink. We need to run when we need to run!

RUN!

Maybe there's a hungry lioness behind us, but do we 'know' that? Or do we just know, RUN!, because that 'lion,' to us, it's not a 'lioness,' it's 'RUN!'

RUN RUN RUN! Until we don't have to run, because, well, because we're not running. There is no 'because.' We won (we're alive), but we don't know that. We don't even remember being chased. Being chased is in our past. We don't have a past. All we have is this 'moment.'

The question is, when we find our way back to the herd, and the herd is crossing a river, all in one graceful, awesome, Africa savannah herd movement, is it a 'river' we cross?

If, with no awareness of past, or future, unaware of anything but the instant moment, can we cross any 'river' at all? Or is this 'river' no more than a watery 'moment'?

Is there any way for us, an existence knowing only the instant-moment, to experience a world of disparate 'things' at all? Or do all things, in a sense, become one thing?

A field of feeling.

And it may seem, on a common-sense level, that, yes, we the gazelle can differentiate 'things' like, say, lions, because we were running from one! We, somehow, knew to do that. But, on another level, there really wasn't a 'lion.' There was a feeling, a feeling genetically honed over untold generations, and that feeling, like wanting to eat when feeling hungry, that feeling said 'RUN!'

There was no 'lion.' There was a feeling. There wasn't even a 'feeling of a lion.' There was just RUN!

'Run' was the feeling. The feeling of hunger is hunger. The feeling of a need to run is a need to RUN!

We, we humans of this world, we grow up differentiating. Primary colors. Shapes. People. Daddy! Every 'thing' becomes its own 'thing.' With a word. Red.

Round. Triangle. Pizza! It becomes the only world we see. A sea of 'things.'

Was it always so?

> *The notion of a 'thing' is thus seen to be an abstraction...[a 'thing'] does not and could not exist apart from the context from which it has thus been conceptually abstracted. And therefore the world is not made by putting together the various 'things' in it*

—David Bohm (1917–1992)

There is a box we build; at some point each of us, in the act of 'learning' how to *be* ourselves, builds this box. That box is the circle, as I'd described it earlier, drawn in the sand of Life. Inside that box is 'me,' outside is 'not me.' And we continually build this box, we continually change this box, as we continually define and re-define ourselves in relation to our world. 'Young me' becomes 'old me'; 'single me' becomes 'married me'; 'me with a daughter' becomes 'me with a daughter and son-in-law,' and so on. Changes continually changing.

I have a son who talks about the day he 'woke up.' He remembers it. He was in preschool, maybe three-years-old, and his daddy, me, came to pick him up. He was already awake, not napping, but he talks about seeing me across the room and 'waking up.' He still knew everything, his dad and mom and teachers and so on, his house and room, but it was like, to him, that he was seeing it all with different eyes, new eyes, and that his life before that moment, who he was before that moment, was lost. Like waking from a dream.

I think the same thing, or similar, happened to me that day my mom told me, "But Johnny, I'm the only mommy you've ever had."

We were, each of us, building our box, and at some point we had to fit the final brick, that last segment that closes the circle. When we do that, we close ourselves off from all that we were, which is all things undifferentiated, undefined, and in return we become that singular definition that is us, individually: a particle in the wave that is our house of Life.

'Consciousness,' that is, awareness of a 'self'—the feeling of being a self existing apart from all that is not self—that feeling may be nothing more than a byproduct of our human ability to catalog experience. It's a new metaphor: we take the wave of feelings that wash over us, the field of feeling, and we parse it into a myriad of 'particles' of experience, and unto each particle we grant a name (including our own), because that's what humans do.

In the beginning was the word…
—John **1:1**

We name stuff.

The man gave names to all cattle, and to the birds of the air, and to every animal of the field
—Genesis **2:20**

Imagine a convenience store security camera that records its image, but with no time/date 'stamp,' on the image, so no standard way of differentiating any one moment on the playback, from any other moment on the playback. Not entirely useless, but…

To 'remember' something, we need a way to differentiate that something. Saying to our co-worker at the convenience store, for example, "Hey, you know that guy who came in, back, you know, whenever," that's probably not a good strategy for sparking a distinct memory. And even if it does spark a memory, there is no way of ensuring that our coworker's 'guy from whenever,' is our 'guy from whenever.'

"That guy from, oh yeah, *whenever. Sure*, I remember him…" Right.

Cataloging a world of connected 'things,' things sliced from the field of feeling and differentiated based on color, shape, size, texture, density, whether they eat us or not, etc.: it's a human ploy, a life hack, a scheme, for filing, retrieving, and referencing, data.

That's our new metaphor: humans 'tag' experience, by naming feelings. We cross-file those tags and build separate files, calling them things like, 'reporting to the boat for the first time.' And having done that we can remember specifics, and 'assemble' the 'pieces' of the experience, and build a story of it from all those individual 'files' we call 'memory.'

I don't, in fact, recall climbing through the thick, round, watertight, hatch in the submarine's cylindrical hull, and down the vertical ladder that led to 'operations compartment upper level,' but I know I did it, and I can fill in that blank when telling the story. But I do distinctly recall standing on deck at the foot of the ladder, and that sense of awe I had. Because I'd made it, to my first boat. The first time I'd ever been aboard a nuclear-powered submarine.

It was only a moment, a bare few seconds that I stood there, and had I been transferred off the next day, had something happened so that I didn't spend those four years aboard her, my memory of 'reporting aboard' would likely be nothing but a blur. But, having spent those four intense years on that boat I can put together the scene in great detail, not necessarily from the scene as it happened, but from other elements learned over time. I can pull in other memories, and other 'tags,' and experience again the squeezed spaces of that boat, the narrow passageways, close ceilings, the sturdy, solid, isolated, feel of her. A descent through a round hole in the water, into another world.

I can imagine the faint hydraulic/mechanical smell, not unpleasant; the gentle hum of ventilation fans; the painted wireways in the overhead, piled high with armored wires leading, like tentacles, everywhere; and underfoot, blue, vinyl, flooring, scrubbed-clean, seamlessly glued to steel deckplates. 'Control' was to the left and ahead as I turned around at the base of the ladder, the tiny 'nucleonics lab' behind a door in front of me, 'radio' behind, 'sonar' and 'supply' down the narrow passageway to the right. At the end of that passageway, almost hidden in the far shadows and up a short ladder, was a thick, heavy, watertight door, a small, oval portal into the labyrinth of reactor compartment, machinery spaces, and engine rooms that lay beyond.

It's all there, a nearly complete picture in my head built from a few tagged files, ready to be used to fill in blanks from other memories, picking up pieces of memory from here and there, building a scene. Like making a movie from stock footage, it's not that it's not 'real,' but it is a 'construction' nevertheless, a piecing together of disparate parts built over time and filed away, a data compression/retrieval ploy used to fill in the otherwise blank spaces of the distinct memory I call, 'reporting to the boat for the first time.'

Perhaps that's why dreams can be so difficult to remember, and why, for most dreams anyway, they can fade so quickly upon awakening. We don't get to deploy our 'overlay' while dreaming. We don't have that seamless ability, in dreaming, to assign a 'name,' to 'tag' the various experiences. When we awake, and as our dreams come to us, we automatically deploy that overlay, parsing the experience of the dream, assigning 'names' to the various 'bits' of it. But even then, and especially if we're trying to relate the dream to someone else, how many phrases such as, 'it was kind of like,' or, 'it seemed like,' or, 'it was almost as if,' do we use as we unravel the story of our dream? Lots of metaphors there!

Life is a metaphor of itself.

'You,' and 'me,' the sure and unfailing consciousness that we *know* that we are, that consciousness that we *feel*, the unflagging awareness of 'I'? It's a tag, the only tag common to every file, cross-referencing every file to the tag called 'me.'

We're part of that naming overlay of ours. We parse ourselves, we name *ourselves*, and call it, 'me.'

Maybe that's the only real difference between my dog Charlie's memory, and mine. Maybe Charlie's memory is more like that convenience store security camera recording; it just goes back 'in time,' recording the entirety of the scene as a more or less complete, data-intensive stream. But, as humans we have learned, in effect, how to compress that 'stream.' Certain elements of the 'recording,' such as the shelves, the counter, the window behind, etc., are continuous, effectively unchanging. So, in memory we tag those unchanging elements. We wrap them up in files, name those files, 'shelves' and 'counter' and so on, and pull up those files when needed to fill in the blanks as we remember any given scene.

But, what started for humans as merely a data compression scheme, a way of reorganizing our memory to allow more of it...maybe, it became a way for us to re-organize our very world, a way of re-imagining the filed 'things' of memory in different orders, different relationships, building in our head ideas for how to change and re-order our world.

Just a thought.

I kind of think, as a little fun aside, that that event, when as humans we learned to overlay our field of feeling with a field of names, to tag experience, as I put it earlier—including the experience of ourselves—it might be recorded, actually written down.

> *Then the Lord God said, "See, the man has become like one of us, knowing good and evil..."*
> **—Genesis 3:22**

To know 'good and evil' we must first be able to differentiate a good 'thing' from a bad 'thing.' We must be able to 'tag' them. Eve ate the fruit of the 'tree of knowledge of good and evil,' gave some to Adam, and they 'knew' they were naked. They became conscious of self, of that thing we call 'me.'

It's interesting that in the story it was Eve who first ate the 'fruit' of that 'tree' (in quotes, because I interpret the story metaphorically), because isn't it women who give birth, who have a 'thing' inside them that is 'part' of them, but then, isn't 'part' of them? It becomes separate, different. It becomes its own 'thing,' a thing 'apart' from what it once was. One becomes two.

Perhaps it was as simple as naming that 'thing,' that thing that was part of her, but now wasn't part of her.

Baby.

I read 'Eve' as a metaphor for all womankind. And isn't it interesting, as well, that it was a 'snake' that put the 'idea' in her, in the first place?

Get the picture?

There may well have been, once upon a time, a kind of tribal/institutional memory of this, of humans, perhaps over generations, learning to 'see' our world in this new way, learning to parse our field of feeling and tag the pieces with names, and slowly, as a species, developing a more sophisticated memory, and with it an enhanced ability to manipulate our world.

There are other elements to the story, of course, like pain.

In a sense, before our 'Eve' became aware of herself as a singular being, demarcated from her field of feeling, if 'she' became 'aware,' for example, of her big toe, it wasn't 'her' big toe. Which might seem weird, but it was just a feeling, not a feeling that was part of 'her,' because there was no 'her'; there was just a field of feeling. So, if she stubbed 'her' big toe, *'she'* didn't feel pain. 'She' literally didn't, because there was no 'she.'

There was no differentiated thing 'Eve.' There was no 'I' 'feel' 'pain'; there was just 'pain!'

'Pain!' was the feeling.

If there is no 'me' involved in pain, then there is also no indignation: 'Who put that rock there!'

Nor is there fear: 'Is it broken!'

No remorse: 'I knew I should have gone around the other side of the fire!'

No imagination: 'I might not be able to walk down to the lake tomorrow, to go fishing!'

There was nothing but simple pain, no complex meaning involved, just...'toe hurt!,' but without even the 'toe' part, because without that ability to differentiate one 'thing' from another 'thing,' there are no 'things.' There are no 'parts.'

So, when Eve ate of that fruit of the tree of knowledge of good and evil, and then, in the story, when God shows up, it seems like 'He's' angry, but maybe 'He's' just telling it like it is, when 'He' says, "in pain you shall bring forth children."

There's another element too: getting kicked out of Eden. Before Eve became 'Eve,' before she learned to 'tag' her experience, there was no 'right' or 'wrong' way to do—anything. There was never a *choice* she had to make, because there was no 'she' to make them. Genetics made the choices. Human genetic feeling/response mechanisms, honed over millions of evolving years, made the choices. Nature, in that sense, made the choices.

But, having drawn a line in the sand of Life, having demarcated themselves out from the otherwise unending field of feeling that was/is their nature, the 'choices' they made became *their* choices. Their responsibility.

Bold move.

Feelings were now *their* feelings. Desires were now *their* desires. Choices were now *their* choices. And choices, as all of us know all too well, can go very, very wrong.

Life became hard.

In that sense, Adam and Eve didn't get kicked out of Eden; they kicked themselves out of Eden, and they didn't have to walk a single step to do it.

Like I said, just an aside, but I think an interesting one.

In a way, the Adam and Eve story could be read as a 'have it both ways' kind of story because scientists—evolutionists—can look back a few thousands of millions of years and see the beginning of Life, and creationists can look back some few thousands of years and see the beginning of Life, with no contradiction.

According to the evolutionists, Life, the Life we know, took all those thousands of millions of years to evolve. Perfectly sensible.

On the other hand, the Life we know, we can't 'know' it without that awareness of 'it.' Until we could differentiate ourselves from the field of feeling, until we could tag 'me' and understand the existence of a 'me,' there is no 'me'; there is only a field of feeling.

To a dog, there is no 'dog'; there is just that field of feeling. Similarly, before Eve, there was no 'Eve.' And in that sense there was nothing, because Eve...*she didn't exist.*

Alive, awake, and aware, if you have no feeling of a cat on your lap, you have no cat on your lap.

Alive, awake, and aware, if you have no feeling, 'me,' there is no 'me.'

So, that makes sense, too. They're both 'right.' Life started millions of years ago, and Life started thousands of years ago, with no contradiction.

11

Frames

October 2017

Somewhere—we can imagine it—there is a guy on a shaded balcony overlooking an idyllic harbor scene, boats tugging at anchor on crystalline blue waters, under sparkling blue skies.

Of the small craft pulled up on the beach, there is one he shall sail, later.

On the table before him is a coffee, maybe a cappuccino, creamy milk near to overflowing the cup, and a folded newspaper, partially read perhaps (or, nowadays, a phone, with a news app).

Behind him, in the cool shade of the bedroom, is a rumpled bed of thick white sheets, and pillows in wild disarray.

'Why?' you may ask.

To ask 'why' is to ask for a reason. Have we need of one?

Except for the 'no reason' part, call it my version of nirvana. I could live there, on that balcony, for lifetimes I think, contemplating the coffee, the newspaper, the boat and sailing it, the meaning of pillows in wild disarray, the sun the moon the stars, Life, the pleasures of it, the frustrations of it, the reality of it.

There's a reality to sailing. Sailing is a thing of context. Many elements must merge together for the boat to go.

114

Indeed, sailing draws on the disparity between those elements; it exploits the relationship of two mediums, water and air, to itself exist. Without air there is no wind, so no go. Without water there is no steering, so no going where one wishes.

Without the context, the relation of wind to boat to water, there is no sailing. Without the context, the relation of one human to another, there is no meaning to pillows in wild disarray. Without the context, of Life all around, there is no meaning to the newspaper.

We could think of it in terms of 'feeling.' Raw feeling. There is a 'feeling field' saturating that moment. Humidity in the air, felt on the skin. Slight breeze on a cheek. Coffee aroma in the nostrils. Perhaps milk on the tongue, and the play of bitter flavors on the back of the throat. The light, sparkling on the harbor, shadows dancing, cool recesses on the periphery of vision...

We could swim, couldn't we, in such a lake of feeling.

But, big but, is it a good feeling, or a bad?

Pure feeling (if there is such a thing), lacking context, has no 'value.' We don't know, lacking context, if a sensation that could be called 'warm humidity on the back of the neck' should be mildly pleasurable, or indescribably fearful—perhaps the hot breath of a hungry lioness, suddenly breathing down our neck.

It might seem, then, that we have to differentiate 'feelings' as a means of establishing that context. So feelings, then, it would seem, are 'things' we 'process,' and then 'place' in context, establishing their relationship to us, and to each other. Which might then imply that for a gazelle, for example, the 'lioness' is indeed a feeling separate from 'run,' which is separate from 'hunger,' which is separate from 'river,' etc. All of which might seem to make perfect sense, except...

We're slipping back (or being pulled back, I think, by habit of thought) into seeing the vase, while ignoring the faces to either side. We're seeing the particles of a wave and calling them separate from the wave. But they aren't.

115

They can't be separate, and still be the particular 'particles' they are, existing within and inherent to the wave.

Without the one, there is no other.

It's not the mere arrangement of particles that 'makes' a creation, nor is it the shape of the wave, the order of the letters in a book, or the pattern of ones and zeroes in a computer program. A yellow circle of crayon, drawn above stick figures and scribbled green 'grass,' all by itself doesn't make for 'refrigerator art.' It's the totality of experience of that paper, handed to you by a proud child as her drawing, that's what 'makes' it 'art.' (Imagine the feeling of that 'same' drawing, handed to you on a dark street corner, by a hooded stranger.)

Context.

All of which is to say: nothing exists in a vacuum. Put another way, everything exists in context. Put still another way, if a thing exists, there is a reason for it to exist, as it is, where it is, in the condition in which it is.

There is a reason. A contextual reason.

We might split Life into two (because we're human, and that's what humans do as a way of making sense of things), parsing Life into a 'thing' called 'awareness' and another 'thing' called 'creation,' or, we might call these things, 'particle' and 'wave,' or 'vase' and 'faces,' but these things aren't 'two things.' To put it into words that recognize two things, where there is but one (that being 'Life'): An awareness is the creation of it; a creation is the awareness of it.

Think of it like music. We hear it all at once. A band, even an entire orchestra, can be 'shrunk' to the 'size' of a needle, vibrating in a moving groove of vinyl. We place a record on a turntable, needle in groove, and...music!

We could, if we wanted, parse out that music. We could pick out the strings and hear it, concentrate on it apart from the rest, or the piano, or the horns, but to do so requires an overlay. It requires specific knowledge not merely of the strand of sound a given instrument might make, but indeed that the sound we're hearing is made up of different 'things,' different instruments playing together. Lacking that knowledge, there is only...sound! Not a collection of things making sound, just, *sound*, vibrations, felt in the ear.

Like language. Upon first hearing a foreign language, do we hear 'words'? Or is it all just a string of sound, a field of feeling of sound, heard as a voice? Lions roar. Birds chirp. Humans speak. All the same. We may know it's 'speech,' but until we can parse it out, overlay it, learn it, bit by bit, it's just...sound...coming from a human.

In that sense, then, and to put it another way: The response to a feeling, *is* the feeling. To feel the 'sound of music,' is to feel sound, heard as music. And while, from a causational perspective, it makes no sense to say that the response to a feeling is the feeling, from another perspective splitting Life into two makes no sense, either.

To separate 'response' from 'feeling,' is a little like splitting a pool ball into two causational entities, one that 'feels' the cue ball, hitting it, and another that 'responds' to the cue ball, hitting it.

A pool ball is all one thing. There are no 'pieces' to it. So, splitting a pool ball into smaller causational pieces only makes sense if we split it along molecular, or atomic lines. Splitting a pool ball atom for atom, we can then talk of each atom interacting with other atoms in a cascade of interactions influencing the entirety of the pool ball, 'causing' it to behave in a coherent manner.

We're not pool balls; that's the counter-argument. We're living beings with 'free will.' And for a living being, there is (1) a feeling, and (2) a response to that feeling: that's the way we've traditionally looked at it. And, in between the feeling and the response (at least for 'conscious' feelings), there is a 'me' doing the responding; we take the measure of what we feel, and consciously respond in a way that seems most appropriate, exercising our 'free will.'

117

Which, interestingly, leaves us with not two 'things,' feeling and response, but three: feeling, response, and that special thing, 'me,' that we each call ourselves.

Awareness, creation…Life.

Looked at that way, we exist as the relationship between feeling and response. And that relationship that we exist as, is named (by us humans). It's called: 'pleasurable waft of warmth on the back of a cool neck,' 'sailboat,' 'coffee cup.' Pillows.' 'Me!' Experiences, all. Experiences are feelings, parsed. And feeling is…

Us. Individually.

When we parse our own self into a 'thing,' that 'has,' feelings, we create, artificially, a boundary that doesn't exist. It's like a marble statue (albeit, one that can talk) saying it 'has' marble. It's not that it *has* marble; it's that it *is* marble. And in that same way, we don't 'have' feelings; we *are* feelings.

Even the feeling of being 'wrong' is a feeling. Maybe that 'pleasurable waft of warmth on the back of a cool neck,' an instant later is felt as the hungry breath of a lioness. Or, maybe, as Nirvana, herself (or himself, your choice), having arisen from that rumpled bed, letting us know, perhaps, that she (he) has…

Life *is* feeling. And the feeling we have, *is* the response to it. Feeling is a verb. To feel 'hunger' is to *be* 'hungry.' To feel 'me' is to *be* 'me.' Even the feeling of a hot cup of coffee, sitting on the table in front of us? It's a verb, because we *are* seeing it, with our eyes. We are smelling it, with our nostrils. We are feeling it, with our fingers, or on our tongue as we take a sip.

> *"A gold medal is a wonderful thing. But if you're not enough without it, you'll never be enough with it"*
> **—Irv (played by John Candy), in *Cool Runnings* (1993)**

Just as a little change of pace, but, was Deep Blue a 'different' computer after it beat Garry Kasparov? Did success 'change' it? It was 1997 and Kasparov (at the time the reigning world chess champion), played a specially configured computer called 'Deep Blue.' It was a regulation match, and the computer won.

Was it a different computer/program after it beat him?

After winning a gold medal in the Olympics, a blue ribbon at the fair, a red sticker in class, or even after we score the last slice of pie in a midnight raid on the fridge and eat it right out of the pan (so proud), are we, having done those things, are we something different, something we wouldn't be, if it weren't for our 'free will'? Or are we, and just like any coffee cup, or sea anemone, or cobalt-60 atom, are we just doing what we do, being what we are, within the context we find ourselves?

Does a downhill racer, poised at the ready in the starting gate of her Olympic event, is she striving to be someone *different*, as she skis the course? Or is she striving to be the most perfect downhill racing version of herself that ever she could be?

Can we, NOW, in the moment, in the right here, right now, is it possible for any of us to be anything other than what we are?

We tend to look at free will as the act of doing something that otherwise wouldn't be done. That pie, for example, we saw it in the fridge, sitting there alone on the shelf almost like beckoning to us, and we did it; we 'told' our arm to do something that otherwise wouldn't have happened, and grab that pie. Isn't that how we look at it? 'We' tell 'ourselves' to do something, and 'we' do it?

Are there two separate 'we's'? Is there one 'we' doing the telling, and one 'we' doing the acting? Is there a kind of overlord 'me' that gives the orders, 'causing' underling 'me' to do something it otherwise wouldn't do?

Isn't that kind of how we look at it? That we live a kind of 'me' (that has free will) within 'my body' (that carries out my free will) existence? So, then, 'my body' (carrying out my orders) is separate from 'me' (doing the ordering), just like 'my world' (pie in fridge) is separate from 'my body'?

Is there a difference in the separatenesses? Are 'we of free will' less separate, or more separate, from 'our bodies' than we are from 'our worlds.' We don't control all our body, do we? Aren't there vast reaches of it, of those 30 *trillion* cells, over which we have no control? And aren't there vast reaches of 'our world,' just the same, metaphorically speaking, over which we have no control?

Is there a difference, then, in terms of how separate we are, between our body, and our world?

And, if there is a separate thing 'me,' apart from 'my body,' then, what is it? What is this 'separate' me?

Soul?

I did mention, didn't I, that one of the metaphors of my life was the blurring of boundaries? (See Chapter One.)

Ever seen the painting with the words (in French), *'This is not a pipe,'* written as part of a painting...of a pipe?

René Magritte painted it. Did he paint a 'pipe'?

The Treachery of Images, oil on canvas, 1928-'29

What if, instead of picking up his paintbrush, Magritte had run down to the hardware store, bought a hammer, mounted it securely to a flat panel, framed it, and written below it, 'This is not a hammer'?

Would that be accurate? Is it a hammer?

Is a framed 'hammer' hanging on a wall in an art gallery a 'hammer'? Can we use that 'hammer' to bang a misaligned metal fence post bracket, for example, into place?

Is the USS Constitution, launched in 1797 and docked in Boston Harbor, is it a warship? It floats. It sails. It has guns. It's a commissioned ship in the actual U.S. Navy. Or HMS Victory, in Portsmouth, UK, launched in 1765, is it a warship? It's permanently drydocked; it will never float again, but it has guns too, and, impressively, it's the official flagship of the First Sea Lord.

But, really, is a boat that can't float even a 'boat'? If it can't float, why would it be called a boat, or ship? How can a 'flagship' not be a 'ship'?

Silly questions?

Frames are funny things. Once we put something in a 'frame,' once we *define* something, it becomes, in our minds, and more or less permanently, that something. Frames separate. Frames are the way we define our world. It's the overlay over our field of feeling, a series of frames, framing the barking dog, or the table that is hard, and framing them so completely, so thoroughly, that even an upside-down dining table is still a dining table despite that eating at it might prove problematic, and a boat is still a boat even if it's not floating, can't float, and never will float again.

How does that work? Story. Interpretation. As long as we see it as a 'boat,' it is a 'boat.'

As long as we see it as a hammer, even mounted on a wall and called 'art,' it's a hammer. Painted on canvas, even if you can't smoke anything with it, even if it *says* it isn't a pipe, in our heads, yeah, it's a pipe.

What have we been smoking, to make that so?

Language.

Once we identify a thing, and name that thing, we can talk about that thing, and place that thing in our mind as an experience of that thing.

But there is an utterly unavoidable, all but unseen handicap to parsing feelings and naming them as 'things.' Because when we frame a thing, when we corral it, and tag it with a name, we remove 'it' from its context.

HMS Victory, of such storied history, Nelson's own flagship at Trafalgar, never again will she heel to an ocean breeze, weather a storm at sea, shield her crew from battering waves or fearsome cannon-fire, but yet there is no denying, she is that proud thing a *ship*, a ship of war.

But, what about that little item, context?

Was Deep Blue, truly, was it the 'same' computer after it beat Garry Kasparov, as it was before?

If we draw a line around it, yes, it certainly was, and is, the 'same' computer. But, and this is the 'truly' part, would it be an exhibit at the Computer History Museum, like it is now, in Mountain View, California, if it hadn't won? If it didn't beat Kasparov?

It's a real question. Has it changed? The 'thing' itself, that thing drawn apart from its context, it's still the 'thing' it was. But, remove that definition, remove that line in the sand separating Deep Blue from not Deep Blue, and realize that *it is the context itself that defines Deep Blue.*

Deep Blue, our definition of Deep Blue, it only exists as 'Deep Blue' because we draw a line around it. But we can only draw the particular line around it that we do, because of the context, because of what 'it' 'did.' Lacking that context, Deep Blue is not 'Deep Blue.'

It's not that we, as humans, can never change. Because we do change. All the time. It is that the change that happens to us, happens within and as part of our context. Put another way, we can only be 'who we are' until, in being who we are, we become something else.

Definitions—frames—corral ideas. They fence them in. We label those corralled ideas, burn that label into the fence of them, so to speak, and call it a 'name.' That's what humans do, all of us; we label ideas, tag experience, parse feelings. And that labeled world, it becomes for us the world we see and respond to—our world, our story, our interpretation.

Peek over the fence holding the definition of 'thing,' and see corralled there (among other ideas) the very idea of 'being' and 'existence.' Do the same for 'context,' peer over the fence walling it in, and see there the *inability* to 'be' apart from.

To 'be,' is to 'exist.' To exist is to 'feel'...something. It's to interact with something. That 'something' is the context of existence. We can't exist outside a context. Put more simply, there must be 'something' for us to 'feel,' or we're not 'feeling' anything. Put another way, if there is no context for an existence, there is no existence.

Context, then, describes the inability to be apart from *oneself*. We are, each of us, our own context, our own 'medium,' in a sense. But we are also our own 'thing' existing of itself.

Yeah, contradictory. But, again, it's the 'look both ways' metaphor. We are a vase, existing only because of the faces to either side that 'form' it. And those faces to either side of the vase, they only exist because of the vase. The vase outlines the faces. Each 'forms' the other. Faces linked to vases, so closely, that the 'link'—poof!—vanishes.

So here we sit, at this table that is hard, hearing a dog that is barking...barking...

Particles of consciousness? Is that what we are?

A soul? Is that our 'true' nature?

A kernel of 'being'? Is that us? Bound, in some way, to a 'body' that is not the kernel, existing on a planet that is not our 'body,' part of a solar system that is not our planet, in a galaxy that is not our solar system, in a universe that is not our galaxy, all perhaps ruled or ordered by a 'god' separate from our universe?

Is that it? A series of...separatenesses? Linked to each other by 'laws' of gravity, and charge, and mass and energy, time and length, and on and on. Is that it?

Because that is, isn't it, more or less the traditional view?

I've been working—going back to that old 'house of Life' metaphor from Chapter One I've been working— to get us to see ourselves, each of us individually, in self-defined terms, as beings existing within and, indeed, because of, a context that itself helps shape that self-definition we are. A kind of detected particle within a wave of detected particles existence.

A little weird. Sorry about that. But the idea is to wean us of this notion that we exist entirely separate from our context. Wean us, in short, of the notion of 'soul.'

Sorry about that, too.

Because it's a compelling notion, right? Soul? If we have a soul, then this ashes to ashes, dust to dust existence? It's not us. And that, by itself, is compelling, because there are so many not-so-nice things about this existence. Doesn't it seem that way to you? And 'soul,' having an existence separate from all those not-so-nice things, it grants us a kind of 'higher being' 'transcending' this 'mere' earthly existence. There's a beauty, an elegance to 'soul.' The word itself, s-o-u-l, saying it aloud, it speaks, to me it does, of a kind of pure beingness, an opaque, transcendent essence that IS what we ARE.

Right?

A core of pure, peaceful spirit: it's a meltingly beautiful, compelling idea, isn't it?

My mom used to call me a romantic. And I was, because my mom was. I was her eldest. We were best friends, back when I was in diapers, hanging out together constantly. As I grew older, and came to know the things she liked, I grew to like the things she liked. She liked candlelit dinners, so I liked candlelit dinners. She liked that quiet moment on Christmas Eve when all the gifts were wrapped, and the tree was decorated, and with *Silent Night* slowly playing on the record player, you sat with your hot cocoa and heard the delicious sound of...peace.

She liked that, so I liked that.

I still like that. I like it a lot.

Aren't all children, at heart, romantics? Don't we all, as children, somewhere inside us, have that gentleness of spirit that wants to see all the world, everything, put right? And, indeed, holds that certain knowledge that it *can* be put right?

Do we have to give that away, when we grow up?

Is that what it means to 'grow up'? To give that away?

When we parse out 'soul,' when we 'fence' it in, when we corral that gentleness of spirit and burn the name of it, 'my soul,' into the fence we put around it, we remove it from its context. It's a part of us, but, apart from us.

It's separate.

Like a 'ship' that will never sail again, forever drydocked, that's what fencing 'soul' can do. It can divide us from our own notion of who we are. And having done that, it allows us to pretend that there's somewhere, somehow, a 'better me.' It allows us to say things like, 'Okay, maybe I did that, but, that's really not me. That's not who I am. *I'm not that person.*'

And if we can hide, even from ourselves, if, happy in the knowledge that we have this thing our own 'soul,' the essence of who and what we are, tucked safely away, if we can say to ourselves that 'the me who I am is not really who I am,' then we can deny that the world around us, is 'our' world, because 'our world,' that thing we 'truly' are, it's called 'our soul,' and we have it tucked safely away.

Such a soul, so drydocked, never will it heel joyously to Life's fair breezes, weather with dignity Life's storms,

shield us, carry us, inspire us to greatness through hard-
ship and trial. How can it? It's corralled. Drydocked.
Fenced in.

Crack open that 'kernel of being' you call yourself.
Free 'transcendent essence' from the corral you've built
around it. *Unleash your soul.*

Let it go…free.

Let it be a part of you in every part of you. Let it suf-
fuse your thoughts, your being, your world. Let it be all
you see, all you know, all you are. Let it be everywhere
at once, and nowhere in particular. Let it be unnamed,
unrecognized, unmistakably *you.*

That's our new metaphor.

Aren't we, all of us, children of our own context?
Don't we define ourselves, and don't others define us, in
terms of where we live, where we work, who we associate with, what we wear, what we drive, the 'context' of
our lives? What color our skin is? What church we fre-
quent? What side of a political line in the sand we were
born on?

And if that's the case, if others are defining us, if we
are defining ourselves, in terms of our context, then,
where is the border between me, and not me? If I am
my job, then those 11-hour shifts, the experience of it,
becomes me. If I am 'white,' then skin color becomes
me. If I drive a 20-year-old hatchback with a broken air-
conditioner, if that's part of my life in California inland
valley summers, that becomes me, part of who and what
I am.

Where does it end? Where does the line in the sand
end? We read about broken lives in bombed-out cities
on the other side of the planet, and aren't those feelings
we have about those broken lives, the broken cities,
aren't those feelings now part of us, individually? Our
house of Life?

Where is the border?

And a sunset over the Pacific Ocean, the feeling of it, the joy of a laughing toddler, the warm hug of a friend, the leaves of autumn on shaded country roads, the lights of the big city, concerts in the park, ice cream, lazy bike rides, watching kids' movies *with a kid*, the smell of barbecue, the *Milky Way!* on a clear, moonless night, seen from a ship's fantail, underway on the Caribbean Sea...

Where is the border?

If everything I experience is/becomes me, then, where is the border? Where do 'I' end?

Sorry to sing the same refrain over and over, but that's it. That's what I've been trying to get at. That's what I've been repeating, all along. That's the wave view, the inside-out view.

There is no border.

12

FREE WILL

April 2018

We once 'connected' my dad to the rudder pedals of an ultralight airplane. He was a tall guy, six-foot, and the not-so-tall guy whose ultralight it was, and who wasn't a pilot, was all fired up about getting my dad to fly the thing, so that my dad could then train him on what to expect when he, the owner, took his first flight in it (that ultralight didn't require a pilot's license). But Dad's legs were too long, and there was no easy way to move the seat. So, under his direction, we strapped Dad's feet to the rudder pedals.

Maybe not a great idea.

The system worked fine—on the ground. Once airborne, however, with a torquey little engine trying to twist the plane over to the left, Dad didn't realize he didn't have enough rudder control to keep the little craft flying straight, until it was too late to do anything but keep climbing...

To the left of the 'field' (a big, weed-covered lot upwind of a four-lane suburban highway) was a long row of trees, and he's banking gently toward them. On the ground, we're wondering what's happening. Sure, he's climbing quickly, but those trees! He'd made some maneuvers we didn't understand; maybe he was just getting the feel of the thing? And it was all in a kind of distant slow-motion, but then it seemed like he was going to make it over the trees, so we're breathing a sigh of relief, when at the last instant, we watched, shocked, as the dipping left wingtip of that little craft scratched the very tip top of the tallest tree in the row.

The treetop swayed as if from a gentle breeze, but the aircraft, with my dad in it, skewed sideways, stalled, and dove, straight down, out of sight on the other side of those trees...

(It turns out, who knew, that bungee cords stretch. That's what we learned, that day.)

Canals crisscross the entirety of South Florida (Fort Lauderdale isn't called the 'Venice of America' for nothing) and we heard a splash, as the engine noise stopped. Sudden silence.

We looked at each other, and I began running, sure he was going to drown. I know he's strapped in. Not just seatbelts, but to the rudder pedals! Those bungees! Visions of my dad, desperately struggling, underwater, are filling my head as I run.

On the other side of the canal was a housing development, manicured lawns shining bright green under lush, sub-tropical, skies. So, that's what greeted me as I *burst* through the underbrush, ready to dive headfirst into the water! But!

No Dad! I'd managed to misjudge where he'd gone down! I looked around to get my bearings and there, standing on the other side of the canal in her own bright green backyard, some few dozen feet upstream from me, was a little girl. She was, maybe, eight, and she said, oh-so-innocently, in her perfect little-girl voice, "Hi!" But, not to me.

Out of breath, wide-eyed, I peered around the row of trees, and there was Dad, on his feet, in the middle of the canal.

Now, when it came to kids, Dad always had a soft spot. He enjoyed play with them on their level, and had fun with them, but he also, and always, took them seriously. To him, they weren't 'kids'; they were full-fledged humans deserving of the same respect and attention he might give any adult human, and often, more. (He also had a thing for cats. Strays. Of those around his warehouse, he always had a favorite, and would save food for it, and feed it, and name it, and call me up to brag of his latest successes in trying to make friends with it.)

Fully clothed, sopping wet, up to his thighs in brackish canal water, he turned and faced her. "Hi," he said to the little girl, taking her seriously.

"What are you *doing*?"

Sticking up out of the water next to him was an ultralight tail. Smiling widely, he said, "I think I just bought an airplane!"

True story. And, miraculously, other than a split in a wooden propeller blade—it hit the water, spinning—we could find no damage to that tough little aircraft.

So, what does that have to do with anything? Free will.

If Life is a feeling—and almost from page one that's what I've been saying—if we are a *feeling*?

Where's the free will in that?

Bungee cords stretch (we actually did know that). That's what makes them so useful. As we rigged up those bungees, on that ultralight, on the ground, what we didn't take into account was that the rudder was going to take a lot more force to move once the craft was flying, at speed, air rushing past.

Stupid, sure. Bad idea, YES! But that rudder? It only did what rudders do, and right on down to the atomic level. 'Things' always do, *can* only 'do,' what they do, being what they 'are.' I've said it before: everything exists in context. Put still another way, if a thing exists, there is a reason for it to exist, as it is, where it is, in the condition in which it is.

There is a reason. A *contextual* reason.

Being what they are, within the context they find themselves, things do what they do. The rudder 'did' what it had to do, being what it was. The engine 'did' what it had to do, being what it was. The airframe 'did' what it had to do, being what it was.

The question is (big question here), did my dad too, did he do what he had to do, being what he was?

'Conscious response': that phrase more or less encapsulates our traditional 'free will' metaphor. We consciously 'cause' our own actions, in effect intervening in the causational workings of the universe. We dam a creek, for example, to irrigate a field so crops can grow where crops otherwise would not grow. And sure, a beaver might dam a creek, too, but there's a difference, as we tend to look at it, because the beaver is not doing it 'consciously.' With the beaver, it's 'automatic'; it's an automated response, a genetic thing, because that's what beavers do, they dam creeks. And that's the difference, as most of us look at it, between a beaver dam and a human dam. They do it automatically, unthinking. But we do it consciously. We do it with intent. We do it for a reason, 'knowing' (we hope) what we're doing.

We're special, in that regard. We're different. We don't even need to be taught it, because we see it ourselves. When our mom pushes the doggy, tail between its legs, out the door into the cold because it did something bad? The doggy, poor doggy, doesn't make a fire in the backyard to keep warm. Doggies don't know how to make fires. Humans make fires. Humans make rocket ships to the moon.

We're special—we're different—we *know* that. But, are we so different —another big question—are we so overarchingly different that we exist apart from the very context of Life? Are we so different that we exist outside the normal parameters, outside the domain, of Life?

Are we that special?

Butterflies are special. Giraffes. Hummingbirds. Sea turtles. Sea anemones. Holly trees. Orangutans. Roses, by any name, are special.

Life, each element. Is. Special.

Funny to look at it this way, but for all that an atom, any atom, is just a thing, with no real 'choice' (as we tend to look at it), it turns out that its individual behavior, in all respects, cannot be predicted with absolute certainty.

Cobalt-60, for example, has a half-life of 5.2714 years. It's unstable, radioactive; it decays into nickel, and at a predictable rate. So, assuming a year is 365.4 days, and starting with exactly one gram of cobalt-60 (don't put it in your pocket), 5 years, 99 days, 4 hours, 4 minutes, and 10 seconds later, there will be precisely one-half gram of cobalt-60 remaining. It seems then that cobalt-60 atoms can be predicted. Indeed, wait that long again, and there will only be one-quarter gram of cobalt-60 left, and that long again and one-eighth gram, and so on. Perfectly, seemingly, predictable.

But, if you have just one cobalt-60 atom? A single atom? When will it decay?

It's like my wife; when will she leave the office, and come home? There is no way to know. Not ahead of time, there isn't. Even if she says she's leaving 'in a few minutes,' even if she says she's *'leaving now,'* that is no guarantee, of anything. It just…it doesn't work that way. Not with my wife it doesn't.

So, I actually don't see much difference between my wife, in that regard, and a cobalt-60 atom. Both are going to do what both are going to do; both will do it when they are good and ready to do it, and not an instant before; and, with both, there is no telling when that 'good and ready' will be—probably even for them. The choice isn't made until the choice is made. Because, if cobalt-60 is anything like my wife, just like my wife can't predict with anything approaching certainty her own behavior (insofar as 'leaving the office'), so too a cobalt-60 atom probably couldn't tell you when it will decay, either, until it actually has decayed. (Whatever did happen to Schrödinger's cat?)

Life is a metaphor of itself.

Given enough time and study, in a given context and with a large enough sample we can predict with high accuracy what percentage of people will take the left fork in a road, and what percentage the right, and how many will pull over and look at a map, and how many will get out and ask directions, but we can't predict, with any certainty at all, what any *one* person, faced with that set of choices, will actually do.

We won't know what that person will do; we can't know what that person will do, and indeed, even the person won't know the choice she/he will make, and *can't* know the choice she/he will make, until the choice is, actually, made. (Or, have you never, unexpectedly, changed your mind at the 'last instant.') Until it is experienced/observed the choice has not been made, and cannot be known.

Life is a metaphor of itself. And, metaphorically speaking, a cobalt-60 atom? It's part of the domain of Life, just as we are. The only real difference between the 'inanimate objects' of our world, be it an ultralight, a fission reactor, or a pool ball, and Life?

There is no difference. They are Life. All 'things' are.

1+1=3.

No?

In the world of dimensions, actually, not 'no.'

As a silly little demonstration (and this only works if you have two good eyes), close one eye, and keep it shut. Having done that, take a look around, and pick out a small target for you to touch. A corner of an envelope, the far rim of your coffee cup. Something within reach but the farther away, the better. And now, touch it, come straight down on it to touch it with the very tip of your finger.

Did you get it, on your first try?

Bet you didn't.

Silly child's trick, sure, but the world we see with one eye, is not the world we see with the other eye—different view, from a different angle—and it is certainly not the world we 'see' with two eyes. 1+1=2? No. 1+1=3...*dimensions.*

Call it the arc of space.

With two eyes, we see—we feel—those three dimensions of space. We can extrapolate three dimensions using one eye; we can abstract that third dimension in our head, in the sense of knowing it's there, but unless we have two good eyes, used simultaneously, we can't visually experience the arc of space.

Remember our imaginary gazelle? That gazelle, at least as we imagined her, she lives, in a sense...forever.

That's her experience of 'time' because for her, there is—literally—*no* 'time.' No past; no future.

I can imagine that Eve, our metaphorical Eve from *Genesis*, before she was 'Eve,' it's likely that she too only had a rudimentary sense of 'time.' For her there just was...what was.

Life in the instant-moment.

But then our metaphorical Eve had her revelation, her epiphany, and saw this infant that was her, but then wasn't her. It was separate from her. And this big, bold, concept, so simple for us, but so revolutionary for her, it allowed her, in her mind, to place a frame around 'Baby.' Baby was now a 'thing,' special, different, separate. And Baby did what babies do.

It grew.

I wonder if that, really, is where we get our own notion of living in 'time.' We get it from the notion of 'existence across contexts,' because when we frame a
thing—when a ship is a ship even when it's bolted to a
concrete foundation—when Baby is still Baby, with a
beard, these things exist, in effect, across 'moments.'

It's such a common-sense concept for us, but a river,
being the *same* 'river,' raging in a flood, and nearly dry in
a drought? A tree, being the *same* 'tree,' a skeleton of
limbs in winter, and dropping ripe fruit in summer? A
baby, being the *same* 'baby'—with a beard? That's a
huge, even revolutionary concept. Indeed, it's the very
concept that builds the notion of 'me.' For all of us.

Separate. From. Context.

So now, our Eve, seeing Baby as a young man, maybe
leaving home for the first time to go on a long hunt,
perhaps she sees him in her mind as that infant, and
comes to understand that this knowledge she has of him
as an infant, is knowledge she acquired 'in the past.'

Baby, as an infant, is 'what was.' Baby as a hunter is
'what is.' And linking those two images, she began to
think, for the first time, in terms of 'what will be.'

And, again for the first time—because she's a mom,
and that's what mom's do—she finds herself saddled with
a new emotion: worry!

Life is hard.

The view of what 'is,' bridged to a view of what 'was,'
grants us the experience of anticipating what 'will be.'

1+1=3: The arc of time.

I've said it before (Chapter Five): just because we can't
put our finger on it, doesn't mean it's not there; and just
because we can put our finger on it, doesn't mean that's
the whole story. Because there is another arc.

The arc of existence.

Currently, we don't see the dimensions of existence.
We can't see them, because one of our eyes is closed.

More than that, the view we see through our open 'eye,' a view of a world of separate things of which we are one of the things, we're so certain it's the 'correct' view that we can't imagine how there could be any other view, at all.

But, there is another 'view.' We do have another 'eye,' another way of seeing our own existence, and from that view, we see the 'field of feeling.'

The field of feeling sees nothing separate. It's a view that doesn't even see 'me.' It's our Eve's view, before she ate of the fruit of the tree of knowledge of good and evil.

Two views. And it's tough to 'see' that second one. But isn't that the conundrum of any two views? Doesn't the left eye see a view that is sometimes so completely different from the right eye, that from the perspective of either eye, the other eye's view must be 'wrong'?

From the perspective of the faces, there is no 'vase.' From the perspective of the vase, there are no 'faces.'

Looking back at what was, we can't see what is. Looking only at what is, we'll never know what was.

It's only when we merge those views together, accepting both as 'valid,' despite that they contradict each other, that a 'third' view can come into focus.

The arc of space. The arc of time. The arc of existence.

When we take our view of ourselves as individuals separate from context, and interweave it with a boundaryless view that recognizes no context, no boundaries, no separatenesses...

When side-by-side we place our disparate views of Life, and, simultaneously, take them in...

"I like this car a lot better, now that it's mine."

My son said that to us, his mom and I, just the other day as I write this. It was kind of a great moment. A few days earlier we'd given him his mom's old car, after having bought for her a newer one. So now her old car, 11 years old, was his new car—his first car—and while he'd never liked her old car, at all, and indeed hadn't really wanted it, now that it's his new car, all his? He likes it, a lot!

Funny how things work out that way, isn't it? Once we take ownership of a thing, metaphorically or otherwise, we see it in a new way, in a new light.

Maybe we can do that with Life. Because the border between 'me' and 'not me,' when we look at those two views together, seeing them side by side, that border—poof!...

It vanishes.

The boundaryless view, that's the field of feeling, that's the 'instant-moment,' the 'moment-eternal' that recognizes no boundaries, no borders, no delineations at all.

It's like an orchestra, but sized on a universal scale. All the horns, the drums, the violas and violins, they all merge into one moment of sound, heard not as violas or violins, but as *music*, All at once. A moment-eternal.

That's the field of feeling, a moment of feeling 'heard,' lived *as* existence. All the 'instruments' heard as one, merging into a single NOW, a single point of *feeling*, a single point that is...itself...

Itself.

Life *is* feeling.

And feeling is response.

Our traditional view of 'things,' that view so familiar to us, of kids and dogs, house and car, holly trees, coffee cups—each of those 'things' is an instrument in the orchestra that is our NOW. Each of those 'things' only exists—as it is, where it is, in the condition in which it is—in relation (particle/wave) to the 'thing' experiencing it, NOW, the thing that we each call 'me.'

To get to the crux of the matter: To experience that 'me' that we each of us are all so familiar with, *while also experiencing the moment-eternal*, when we do that, we experience ourselves as boundaryless. To merge those views, and to put this another way, is not to be a 'me' existing 'in' a field of feeling; it's to be a 'me' that *is* the field of feeling, *all* the field of feeling, *all* the moment-eternal, *all* the boundaryless whirl—that's what we are.

Our brain, it works in certain ways. It jumps to certain conclusions. It likes its shortcuts! So, it tends to jump to familiar thought encapsulations, and phrases like, 'we're all one' or 'we're all connected,' we've heard such things before. So we tend to jump to those kinds of understandings. But that's not the jump we want to make.

To be 'connected' implies separate 'things' 'connected' 'together.' But in the boundaryless whirl, there are no separate things to be connected. Nor, and this might seem strange as well, but this existence as the boundaryless whirl is not about being all 'one' 'thing' either. Because, again, from this view, *there are no 'things.'*

I've called it the 'wider' self. We could probably think of it as our 'non-conscious' self as well, and I introduced it mostly as the rather dry 'field of feeling,' but I think, with acquaintance, that 'boundaryless' works better: the boundaryless self, the boundaryless moment, the boundaryless whirl. It's the third dimension of existence: we exist, each of us, as boundaryless.

A 'thing' wholly unconfined, even a 'self,' can't exist. It isn't a 'thing' if it's unconfined. But this boundaryless thing that is our self, that is itself not a thing? It brings us back to the house of Life, particle/wave, look both ways, vase and faces, 1+1=3: all the metaphors come into play. We're looking at two things at once, focusing on neither alone, and seeing a third thing entirely.

It's not a 'model' of Life that we're building; it's a view of Life that we're mapping. What we experience is what we are, and in being what we are, we, serendipitously, and in the fullness of 'time,' can become anything at all.

Put another way, things don't happen to you; *you* happen to you.

...love your neighbor as yourself....
—Matthew 22:39; Mark 12:31; Luke 10:27

When we see it as 'ours,' when we come to terms with the sure knowledge that we are, indeed, all that we experience, every bit of 'it,' maybe, then, like my son suddenly liking his 'new' car, we'll come to see *ourselves* anew, and come to like, and even love, our own 'new' boundaryless self and all those very many, (and usually) very worthy souls with whom we share our boundaryless world. You know who they are. It's your world you share with them.

Just a thought.

Free will? It isn't about 'control.' (What is there to 'control,' in a boundaryless world?) Free will is not an 'act.' It's not something we 'do.' It's the being that *is* that 'act.'

Feeling is the response to it.

An atom of cobalt-60 will act as an atom of cobalt-60 will, just as my dad will act as my dad actually did. Just as each of us will act as we are. Because that's what we are. What we're feeling: that's what we are.

Truth: an honest representation of experience.

Feeling *is* response. And free will? Truly, what is it? It's Life. That's our new metaphor. And Life—to exist, consciously, as Life—is the absolute freedom, responsibility, and indeed privilege—to *be* any symphony, to sing any song...at all.

13

The Song

June 2018

My Uncle Bill, the artist and teacher (he taught at the Art Students League in New York City for nearly 30 years), just since last I wrote of him, he has passed away at 90 years old. Life is change.

The last time we went out to dinner, and it's been several years now (different coasts), but I remember I asked him what he felt as he painted. I thought I could get a sense of what he was 'saying' in his paintings, what they meant...to him. Silly me, because the answer was a complete surprise.

"Nothing," he said. "I strive to feel nothing."

It took me aback.

His wife of many years, my aunt, was with us at the table, along with my grown daughter, all of us eating Italian on a lovely autumn evening. And for some long minutes (and, really, for the rest of that oh-too-short visit), I was actually speechless. All I could muster was small-talk after that.

On the short walk back to their apartment my uncle sent the ladies on ahead and pulled me, unexpectedly, into a liquor store. It was a large liquor store with lots of vertical space, well-lit and gleaming in the Manhattan night-time, and every wall in that memorable shop was decorated in non-stop, floor to ceiling, wine, beer and liquor, bottles of it, cases of it, from all over the world.

His eyes were alight: "Isn't it great!"

We didn't buy anything. He just wanted to show me! He was like an 87-year-old little boy, grinning with big dimples on mischievous cheeks. There was always a kind of carefree, 'let's jump the fence' quality to my uncle, but his art, to him, it wasn't a mischief; it was his life. He absolutely meant it when he said to me, "Nothing. I strive to feel nothing."

I pondered that. And pondered that. An artist, feeling nothing...

I once had a cat on my lap who, no kidding, tried to have her babies there. It was on the very day, the very morning, actually, that my mom died. Not making that up.

I was alone in an apartment I shared with a roommate, sitting in a chair I never sat in, reading a magazine I never read, the same page over and over again. I didn't think anything of the cat on my lap. It was my roommate's cat, but it liked me better than it liked my roommate (cats are cats), so it was always jumping up on my lap. And, yes, we did know she was pregnant. My girlfriend, now wife, and I had set up a little 'nursery' for her in the closet. But she didn't want that nursery. She wanted to be on my lap when she had her babies. I didn't know that part.

At some point I noticed she was squirming, moving around a lot. I lifted up the magazine, a little annoyed with her, and she was looking at me...and oh my goodness, those eyes were big, and so very frightened! Just a few months ago she'd been a kitten; now she was in labor.

It got me out of my funk.

She was a tiny thing, a sweetheart of a cat. My roommate's girlfriend had named her, Terra. He married that girl; I was best man at their wedding. When my wife and

I moved into our first place, they put Terra into our care. She stayed with us for 20 years. She's buried in our backyard, now.

Life keeps moving. Always changing. Always anew. But there is continuity. We're the same person, for a lifetime, despite being a different person every day, even every moment. How? Feeling. It's what we are. The feeling of being you, is you.

We get caught up in 'models.' Frameworks. The 'circuitry' of Life. We want to know: How does Life work? Where does death fit into the 'model'? What buttons do I have to push, what dials do I have to turn, to make me happy?

Physicists think in terms of physics; doctors, medicine; philosophers, reason and logic; the religious, they understand things in terms of 'gods' and morality. It's the old saying, the 'law of the instrument': if your only tool is a hammer, every problem looks like a nail. And certainly we can be flexible about it. We find ways to meld disparate models together. Most scientists, indeed, through history and to this day, for many of them, have been devout in terms of religion. God becomes viewed as the grand architect of the universe, within which science, neatly, fits.

All feeling is valid.

Eve, our metaphorical Eve, when she ate of that fruit of the tree of knowledge of good and evil, oh my, the mischief she wrought!

She gave to us our experience of 'things' spanning contexts, the experience of 'me,' the experience of 'time,' the certainty that there was a 'past,' and that there will be a 'future.' She gave us personal pain, and worry.

She made the choices of Life *our* choices; she made the life we lived *our* Life; the sorrows of Life, they became our sorrows.

And the joys of Life? They became ours, too.

Joy.

Where is the joy, if there is no meaning?

That's what she gave to us, ultimately, meaning. Life became *meaningful*, and through that meaning we could experience joy, not only for ourselves, but for others. Via our shared meaning the joy of others could be our joy too.

The choices we make—about who we are, what symphony we hear, what song we sing—it's those choices that give Life meaning. They give *us* meaning, because they don't vanish into the vacuum of space; they have momentum, so to speak (another metaphor); they live on to become part of our context, part of who we are. Our choices, our context, our worlds reflects who we are, what we are in our boundaryless entirety.

There is one last gift our Eve gave to us. Hidden, sure. And we have to unwrap it but it's there, embedded in all the other ideas she gave to us.

Remember that 'soul' we unleashed? That soul, it's like a song.

I think that sound, any sound, not just music, but music I think captures the idea most clearly, it makes for an apt metaphor of Life as 'feeling.' Sound merges. It melds. All the instruments of an orchestra meld to a moment of sound, a vibration in our ears heard as music.

Feeling too, it merges, it melds, it's 'felt' all at once: the rain outside falling, the fan inside blowing, the kitchen that is hot, the air that is humid, the table that needs clearing, the boss who is demanding, the clothes that need washing, an aunt who needs visiting, the cookies that are calling, the dog that needs walking, the coffee that is cooling, the career that is going nowhere, the spouse you fear is leaving, the children who need rearing, the rent that needs paying, the car that needs fueling, the head that is aching, they all merge to a pinpoint of moment, all heard, seen, felt, thought, tasted, smelled, all at once, all merging to that single moment, a single 'note,' of life, lived NOW.

But that note, it's a moment in a lifetime of moments, a lifetime of notes felt in our head, in our gut, in our senses, in our world. And the next note, and/or the next after that, each new moment, potentially the first in a new lifetime of continuing moments, it can become kids who are great, the rent that can be covered, the aunt who understands, the dog that is sweet, the car that doesn't need a full tank, the boss who can go to a place full of warmth, and let those chips fall where they will, and the spouse who is, well, we can work that through, and a table that was a wedding present from a dear friend, and meant so much to both of you, and the rain, warm and gentle outside, falling on a roof that keeps you dry, in a home that keeps you warm, with running water, and a comfy couch and warm beds, and crayon drawings stuck to the fridge, in a life that is *worthwhile*, that does have joy, that does have promise, that can be worked, that can become great, truly great, because true greatness? It's not about bank accounts, or history books. True greatness, the kind that no history book or bank account could ever hope to reflect? It's about relationships. Our relationship, to our world. All of it.

"Never say never; never say never; never say never again"
—Henri the Pigeon, in *An American Tail* (1986)

Life perfectly creates itself, but Life isn't perfect. Life is Life!

For we humans, we who live our oh-so-encompassing lives, this 21st Century world of ours where we can venture indoors in Miami, and the next time we go outdoors we're in Milwaukee, or Milan, or Mumbai! Some of us do it all the time. Hunger? For a lot of us? It's a 'I'll grab a bite on the way' kind of thing. It's a 'sure I'm hungry, but hunger is not 'me'' kind of feeling.

Or, is it?

Don't you have a hunger?

My uncle did, a hunger to paint. Builders have a hunger to build: houses, or families, or businesses, or an empire! Doctors have a hunger to heal. My wife, she has a hunger to see that the right thing is done, that's her profession. I have a hunger to sing, my ideas. Don't we all have a hunger? To *flower*? To be those things at which we are at our best?

When we are doing those things, those things we are drawn to do, when we are at our most useful, whatever it might be—caring for others, keeping the world in order by keeping the fires lit, or putting the fires out (metaphorical or otherwise), easing another's pain, teaching, organizing, protecting, nurturing, entertaining, *creating that thing*—whatever that thing is that we do feel driven to create, that thing that wouldn't exist if it wasn't for us creating it—even a clean window! It's a creation! They don't stay clean by themselves. And flowers don't have to dazzle, to be wonderful.

Aren't we all, when we're doing that, when we ourselves are *flowering*, isn't it that it's not that we're feeling 'nothing,' but, that we are being 'me,' without feeling that 'me'? That we are being our most self-less selves?

In the act of perfectly being ourselves, the armor goes away. The pretensions go away. The vanities. Not all. And not entirely, maybe, but isn't that what 'flowering' is all about? Being the all that we are, who we are, what we are, what we can be?

Isn't that what 'finding ourselves,' when we're young, is all about? Finding those seeds within us that we can grow, that we can develop into our flowers, into our passions (are we only allowed one, per lifetime?), into a song, into our Life?

My uncle—when he painted—that 'nothing' that he strove to feel, as he put brush to canvas? That nothing was his boundaryless self, the entirety of his song melded, like an orchestra, to the tip of his paint-laden brush. He tried to take the entirety of himself, of what he was feeling as himself, and put it onto canvas, all at once, one moment, one brushstroke at a time.

That's what Life does. Life is a self-portrait, and the portrait, it talks back.

Life is a metaphor of itself.

To be the 'all' of a thing, is to be no one part of a thing. It's infinity/zero.

Feeling, to truly feel the all of Life, the 'self' goes away. The 'agent' goes away. The 'conscious being' goes away. It all goes away.

Life needs no 'boundary.' 'It' is boundaryless. 'It' needs no sense of being, or self, to create itself. Boundaryless creation: that is Life. That's what Life does.

Life, in creating us, creates itself. We, in creating ourselves, create Life. From the bottom up, from the top down, from the sides and corners and walls and floor and ceiling too, Life creates. That's what Life does. The bottom floor of Life generates a new top floor. The old top floor becomes the new bottom floor. We pull ourselves up by our own bootstraps. But how?

Easy! We feel our way!

We make it up as we go along. We really do. Life does too. That's what it is. That's what Life does. Creating as we go. Making it up as we go.

Orangutans, orange trees, sea anemones, sea turtles, slime molds: they do the same, they make it up as they go.

I think, even molecules do. A molecule of silica, for example, it's 'found' a stability of feeling, and *is* that feeling. I think even atoms. Cobalt-60 'found' a stability of feeling, as cobalt-60. But at some point, that feeling? It stops feeling right, so, decay! To nickel! Big jump, for an atom, to become something new.

Sure it's silly. Sure it's simplistic. Atoms, feeling? But that's it, feeling is its own thing. Who are we to judge!

When we develop that passion—mundane, exotic, anywhere in between, it doesn't matter—but when we find that flower that is us, we have unleashed our meaning, our soul, and the song that lives forever.

Some songs are about relationships. But all songs, all of them, *are* relationships. Because, funny thing about songs, but it doesn't matter what note you use to start singing.

You can start a song anywhere, on any note, and as long as you can make it to the next, to sing that next one, and the one after that, and have them be heard, then, it's the same song. High notes, low notes, in between notes: it's not the 'notes'; it the relationships between the notes. That's what a song is.

That's what we are.

Put another way, it's not the 'thing,' it's the experience of the thing. A song is embodied in the relationship of one note to the next. So it's not the 'instruments' that 'make' the song; it's the relationship between the notes the instruments play that makes the song. *Happy Birthday*? It can be played by an orchestra, by a flute, by a guy with a stick hitting a string of beer bottles each filled with varying amounts of beer, causing each to play their own 'note.' Fun.

Sure, the song will 'sound' different, sure it will 'be' different, depending on the instruments, the note it starts on—the context—but still…'same' song. Funny how that works. But the notes, how they're played, the instruments, what they are, it doesn't really matter because in the hands of a great musician, the greatness of a song…it comes through.

We, each of us, are the great musician of our own life. Life is our orchestra. All the many elements of our life, each are an instrument, an 'instrument of feeling,' a particle, in a sense, in a wave of feeling. We place those instruments of feeling in relationship to us, and to each other, based on how we feel about them, based on our 'model' of the world, on our 'judgements' of the world, based on our 'song,' the song we sing, every day when we go out the door of our house of Life.

As we 'see' them, as we understand them, as we build the reasons for our world, making sense of our world, we place some elements 'closer' to us, others farther away, so some play louder, and are more important, and others softer, so less important, and others we 'hear' hardly at all, all as suits us, as what is important to us being who we are as conscious beings, all in the context within which we find ourselves as boundaryless beings.

Together, those instruments of feeling, the elements of our Life, they merge like an orchestra into the symphony that is us, that is our 'feeling' of our world, our feeling that defines us, that IS us—literally, that is us—because we *are* feeling. And feeling is the response to it. In that sense, we are the conductor, playing our song of Life, the song that reflects our meaning, our flower, our soul, who we are. Playing it, and responding to it.

And since songs, like feelings, exist not as the instrument, not as the 'note,' not as unique 'particles,' as 'this' particle and 'that' particle, but as *relationships*...

Just as a song can be heard again, so can we. Again. And again. And again...

That's Eve's final gift to us, that was ours to unwrap.

That song that is us, individually, it is heard as part of the context that we are. And heard, it is judged. Knowledge of good and evil, morality: it all comes into play. The song we are is judged within the context of the song. Judged, as any song is, as one it would be good to hear again...or not.

That song we are, like a plant that needs certain soil conditions to live and thrive, the song we are will only play in a context that allows it to play, in a context that supports it, nurtures it, feeds it. Context matters. The song we are, the song of each of us individually, and no matter the nature of the song, it will only play, it can only play, where it fits, where it is valid, where it is, in effect, 'invited' to play.

The universe is infinite. Infinite Life. Infinite formats of Life. Infinite space. Infinite time. Infinite particles, elements of being. Infinite.

And so are we.

When we unleash our soul, and understand that the thing that we are exists as boundaryless, and that that boundaryless 'thing' exists as relationships, then that order of relationships? It can exist in any format, as any orchestra, any flute, any series of beer bottles. The song that is us, it exists in countless formats, 'covered' by countless existences—a song never-ending.

And yet, end it must. All songs 'end.' They have to end; they have to finish, or it's not a song; it's background noise. Songs are particles, detected elements in the wave of existence. That's what we are; that's what consciousness is, detected existence. So we, the detected particle that is each of us, existing in a context, in the wave of detected particles that is our life, we have to end. The song that we are, it can be played again and again, by different orchestras, in different contexts, in different formats, but each detected 'song,' for it to be a 'song,' it has to end.

'Death' opens the gate of the corral named 'me.'

We share this world that is ours, alone.

On the one hand, the totality that we know as our world exists as a thing that only we, individually, can experience: that's our shared, different world. But, looking at it from the other direction, there is a sense in which each of us, in effect, act as a placeholder for all the rest of us. The world I share with my neighbors my neighbors can see in me, and vice versa. Put another way, we each build for ourselves a world that we then share with others, who experience our world in their own way: I build a boat; we sail in it; you bring the beer; we drink it. In that sense, then, ours is a shared, overlapping world of overlapping experience. As each of us act as an element of the life of all of us, we build…each other.

Even the past—even the world, for example, of George Washington—it's part of who we are. It's a particle in the wave of NOW that we differently share and call 'the past,' a particle not of George himself, necessarily, but certainly of 'George Washington' the metaphor, of a time, a place, a culture, a history, a long and painful and woefully unfinished *transition* from a world of king and subject, master and slave, rich and poor, to a world of citizens equal. He exists, NOW, as part and parcel of that wave of NOW that comprises the ever-changing context of our world.

And again, it's easy to get caught up in the mechanics of it. But, feeling? It's its own thing. It doesn't need a 'medium.'

Patterns of bosons, patterns of accelerations in electro-magnetic fields: this is how we may think of 'feeling,' as how it 'manifests' in our kinetic whirl. But the kinetic whirl doesn't generate feeling any more than feeling generates the kinetic whirl. They 'generate' each other. It's awareness/creation: without an awareness of a creation, there is no 'creation'; without a creation to be aware of, there is no 'awareness.' They are flip sides of the single 'coin': Life.

The 'model' we have of Life, whatever 'model' we have and use of how Life, our life, of how it 'works,' that model *is itself a feeling*. It is itself Life. That model doesn't exist as a thing separate from Life. The model we build of our Life *is* our Life. Part of our Life. The story we build is the story we are. Which is to say, our 'models' are not 'models'; they are us.

Life is a self-painting self-portrait. It paints itself; *we paint ourselves,* individually, because (being boundaryless) we *are* Life. We, each of us individually, the existence

150

we have, the existence we know, it's our own self-portrait. Everywhere we look, we see ourselves.

Humans enslave other humans. To this day we do. *We*
do. Not them. Us. We. Together. It's our shared, different world that does it.

The human power of perseverance, of hope, of
strength, not by the power of arms, but by the power of
faith, in humanity, in Life itself, that's the strength pos-
sessed, most especially, by a human enslaved. In a human
enslaved there must be faith, there must be *hope*, that despite the overwhelming evidence before their very own
eyes, of the cruelty of which their fellow humans are so
deftly capable, that humanity itself, somehow, is worth
surviving for.

Let's not let them down.

In the grand scheme of things, we're really only getting started at being human. We can, if we wish it, have
a long, a very long, way to go, and there is no need for
slavery, poverty, or children lost, to be included in any
part of that journey.

In the end, the enslaved human's perseverance, to *live*,
it should inspire all of us, as brightly as it shines a light on
all of us.

There are many of us who don't think we're special.
There are many of us who are quite certain that they,
and probably all of us, are not special, that there is something profoundly 'wrong' with us. And I'm sure that,
from their perspective, they have a point. We are all,
each of us, valid. But, there are some thirty trillion (with
a 't') cells of our body, of each of us, which, I suspect, if
we let them speak, they would tell us something different.

'We're all in this together': I tell myself that, speaking
to the 30 trillion or so cells that I share with myself. As I
said before, we build this world that is ours alone, together—*including* our cells. They're in on it too, building

us. They/we work hard, so I tell them, *"we're all in this together."*

Silly sure, but…and you have to mean it, of course.

We're still singing. I am anyway. Trying to get you to see, really, me. My take on things.

And probably it is silly, but you might try it someday, saying it to yourself, and really meaning it, believing it, 'we're all in this together,' saying it to the trillions of hard-working cells that are you, that is the thing you must be to live as this kinetic whirl we differently share. And having said that to yourself—and having meant it— if you don't believe your cells are talking to you when a feeling of warmth wells up from somewhere deep inside, then, well, I guess I haven't done a very good job…singing.

The last words my dad spoke to me were heavy with the Philadelphia accent of his youth.

It was late. The lights were off. I was standing next to that tall hospice bed, contemplating…stuff…silent as a mouse as he slept—if you could call that unconscious state he was nearly always in by then 'sleeping.' It had been several weeks, at that point, of him slipping further and further from us, when, "Johnny! Is that you?"

"Hey, Dad. Just…checking on ya."

"It's not right. My brain's not right. I keep seeing colors. It's not working right."

"It's the drugs, Dad. They're taking over. Maybe it's time, you know…to just…let it go."

"Get outta here!"

His reply was loud and clear, and absolutely he meant those words! The last I would ever hear him speak. But I left smiling, because that was Dad! The old Dad, the Dad I knew. And I knew too, somehow, that I'd said exactly what needed to be said. ("Don't *try* to do it, Johnny. Just *do* it!")

Hours later, he was gone.

THE SONG

I flew home the same day Dad passed.

In a lot of ways, it had been a fun trip to Florida, which sounds weird, because we ended up helping guide Dad through what turned out to be his demise, but, we three brothers were together doing it. We live in three different states, far removed from each other, so it was nice to see them. It was nice to go out with them and have some beers, and have common goals, common worries, common chores, common...stuff. All that stuff of Life, and we were all there for each other. Wives flew in. Kids flew in. Cousins we hadn't seen for years flew in. Stepfamily we hardly knew, but got to know better, flew in. People came out of the woodwork to help. People we didn't even know, had never met, and probably never will meet, donated their nearby condo, unused for the summer, for us to stay in for those weeks. Nice condo too!

With my brothers in Florida to take care of things, I booked a flight home the same morning he passed, and within a few hours I was on an airplane. Both the flight to Atlanta, and then the connecting flight home, had assigned seating, and both airplanes were full. Well, almost full, because, strange to say, as full as both those flights were, the middle seat next to my window seat, on *both* flights, was open. No kidding, the only seat on both planes that was open, was the one next to me.

Weird huh? But, Dad always did know his way around airports...

(My story. My song. I'm sticking with it.)

THE END

LUGS

Index

Made in the USA
Middletown, DE
25 January 2019